Talking Funny for Money

Talking Funny for Money

An Introduction to the Cartoon/Character/Looping Area of Voice-Overs

PAMELA LEWIS

APPLAUSE
THEATRE & CINEMA BOOKS

Talking Funny for Money
An Introduction to the Cartoon/Character/Looping Area of Voice-Overs
By Pamela Lewis

Art Direction: Michelle Thompson
Book Design: Kristina Rolander
Cover logo design: Tristan Eaton

ISBN: 1-55783-504-7
Library of Congress Cataloging-in-Publication Data
>   Lewis, Pamela, 1950-
>   An introduction to the cartoon/character/looping area of voice-overs /
>   by Pamela Lewis.
>   p. cm. + 2 cds
>   ISBN 1-55783-504-7
>   1. Voice-overs. 2. Animated films. 1. Title.
PN1995.9.V63 L49 2003
778.5'347 — dc21   2002152459

Printed in Canada

British Library Cataloging-in-Publication Data
>   A catalogue record for this book is available from the British Library

APPLAUSE THEATRE & CINEMA BOOKS
151 West 46th Street
New York, NY 10036
Phone: 212-575-9265
Fax: 646-562-5852
Email: info@applausepub.com

SALES AND DISTRIBUTION:

NORTH AMERICA:
HAL LEONARD CORP.
7777 West Bluemound Road
PO Box 13819
Milwaukee, WI 53213
Phone: 414-774-3630
Fax: 414-774-3259
Email: halinfo@halleonard.com
Internet: www.halleonard.com

UNITED KINGDOM:
COMBINED BOOK SERVICES LTD.
Units I/K, Paddock Wood Distribution Centre
Paddock Wood, Tonbridge, Kent, TN12 6UU
Phone: (44) 01892 837171
Fax: (44) 01892 837272
United Kingdom

Table of Contents

Disclaimer

The voice-over business is subjective and ever-changing. This Workshop, including CDs, Exercise Manual and text, is as accurate as I could make it, but developments may occur after the printing date that make certain statements obsolete. Although I've based my advice on years of experience, it's only my opinion; unfortunately there is no "Book of Rules" for guaranteed success. Carefully weigh all advice and use your own judgment as to its value.

The author and Applause Theatre & Cinema Books shall not be responsible or liable to any person or entity for any loss or damage caused, or alleged to be caused, by the information given in the *Talking Funny for Money* workshop.

To Dan Duckworth, who first asked me,
"Have you ever thought about teaching this?"

Acknowledgments

My deepest appreciation to:

My students, from whom I always learn.

Jennifer Duckworth and Kevin J. Taylor, my gifted producers at Blabbermouth Productions.

Mark Glubke, and all the dedicated folks at Applause Theatre & Cinema Books.

My fellow actors, who allowed their voices to be heard on this CD Workshop.

All the industry professionals who kindly agreed to be interviewed.

My colleagues at Full House Studios, Voice Overs Unlimited, The Brookwood Studio and Ron Rose Productions, who generously share facilities, talent and information, and allowed me to profit from their experience.

Maddie Blaustein, my first character-voice instructor, who inspired and encouraged me.

My extremely tolerant friends and family.

All my voice-over clients who've kept me employed through the years.

And last but not least, a special thank-you to my loving and supportive husband, John Neville-Andrews (who just happens to have a wonderful voice!).

Preface:
Why a CD Workshop?

I've been a professional actor for over 30 years, and I've been able to make my living completely from the cartoon/character/looping area of voice-overs for the last 15 of those. Any voice-over success I've achieved is based on this: I treat every voice-over role that isn't totally "straight" (me speaking in my natural voice), as a "character" (someone completely *different* from me). Even if the role is a perfectly normal human — a doctor, or homemaker, or announcer; not "cartoony" or "funny" in any way — if it's not Pamela Lewis the actor (a middle-aged, transplanted Southerner with big eyes), then I approach that role the same way I would the most exotic cartoon creature. If it's not me, then the character I'm portraying has a different name, appearance, background and, of course, sound. In my mind, a young executive type talking about why you should choose a certain investment company is every bit as removed from me as a talking gerbil, and, therefore, all the audition pressure to "just be yourself" is eliminated. This technique:

 ▸ Loosens me up. (Why be nervous? Nobody's judging *me*!)
 ▸ Gets me out of my own head (so I have some brain cells available for listening).
 ▸ Helps me be an actor who's focused on making sense of the copy, rather than one who's fixated on the sound of her own beloved voice. (I call those people "noises with legs," because they sound as

though they have no soul, and I don't know of anyone who wants to work with them.)

▸ Helps me achieve the state of confident relaxation that books jobs, makes for positive voice-over sessions, and creates repeat clients. (And the next thing you know, you have a career!)

After working in the cartoon/character/looping field for a few years, I was approached about teaching this area of voice-overs to those who wanted to investigate the "fun part of the business." It seemed only logical to base my teaching method on the performance technique that had worked so well for me, so that's what I did in my *Talking Funny for Money* workshops. These five-night intensives — "An Introduction to the Cartoon/Character/Looping Area of Voice-Overs" — have always been very popular; unfortunately, many interested people (particularly those folks who are not already in the acting profession), have a hard time committing to a five-night workshop because of family, job schedules, or financial obligations. A number of these "civilians" have always enjoyed doing funny voices, or love being all the characters when reading stories to their children, or have innately quirky speaking voices and have often heard, "You should do animation." Naturally, these people are curious about just how good they really are, and wonder what it takes to be truly competitive. (After all, it's difficult to know whether you should "give up your day job," when you have very little information about the alternative!) There wasn't a shorter, cheaper, cartoon/character/looping training program in New York that I felt comfortable recommending to people who couldn't take mine, so I thought, "Maybe I should write a book; at least people could read about this very specialized end of the voice-over business." But here's the rub: There are many books on "How to Do Voice-Overs" already available, and while some contain useful information, reading about how to make sounds — rather than taking a workshop where you get verbal guidance, actually make the sounds, and then for comparison purposes hear examples of professional actors doing the same exercise — has always seemed to me "better than nothing," but of limited value when compared to a hands-on experience. I was in the proverbial quandary when Kevin Taylor of Blabbermouth Productions suggested that I record my workshop onto CDs, accompany them with the Exercise Manual used in the live class, and make the package available to those who could never manage the five-nighter.

I was struck dumb by the brilliance of his suggestion. (Well, nearly dumb; totally would have been bad for business!) And with Blabbermouth as my producer, I proceeded to create this CD Workshop. It's the closest possible thing to actually taking my class, and I'm very happy to be able to offer it to you. I trust you'll find it informative, challenging and *fun*! As you'll probably be able to tell, I love my work, and I hope you'll be inspired to join me in the cartoon/character/looping area of voice-overs. As I always say, "What could be better than making funny noises for a living?!"

Please proceed to page 15 to find out "How to Begin this CD Workshop."

How to Begin this CD Workshop

Congratulations on your decision to explore your cartoon/character-voice potential!

This CD Workshop includes:
— 2 CDs
— Text with Exercise Manual

Since a voice-over workshop on CDs with follow-along exercises is a new idea, I've tried to make the learning process as simple as possible. The CDs will instruct you how to begin, and then tell you exactly how to proceed. Occasionally on the CDs you'll hear, "Pause the CD while you try it." You should do just that, for as long as you need to. (The beauty of participating in a class where you control the practice time becomes immediately apparent!) Sometimes the CD will refer you to the text, and vice versa. You'll notice that a section of this book is called "Exercise Manual," where each exercise page is accompanied by a blank area for your notes. This "Exercise Manual" section is meant to separate the class exercises from the remainder of the text (containing marketing advice, professional tips, etc.), which can be read at a later time. Many terms are explained on the CDs, but there's also a more comprehensive "List of Terms" included in the book.

This CD Workshop covers:

▸ How to start from scratch in the cartoon/character/looping area of the voice-over business.

▸ How to assemble a competitive cartoon/character-voice demo.

▸ Shortcuts to getting a handle on the most-requested dialects, age groups and celebrity impersonations.

▸ How to develop a dependable stable of character voices that will help you "control" an audition (in a nice way, of course!), and reassure potential clients that you're an old pro at this.

▸ Film looping/dubbing "technique and terminology" (including information on loop-room procedures and sound editor requirements).

▸ How to increase your vocal variety and stamina so as to appear more "cost-effective" to a tightly-budgeted potential client.

▸ "Where do I put my funny voices other than in cartoons?" Information on the wealth of varied employment opportunities in the cartoon/character/looping world, and tips on how to market yourself.

Whether you're already gifted with vocal variety, a hard worker who wants to expand your casting potential, or just someone who's been told "You have an interesting sound," this skills-enhancement program could be exactly what you need. Good luck!

To find out what it takes to enter this creative and lucrative area of voice-overs, BEGIN CD #1.

CD Workshop Track Listing

CD #1

Track 1: Section #1 Introduction: What is the Character/Cartoon/Looping Area of Voice-Overs?

Track 2: Section #2 Introduction: Why Do Cartoon/Character/Looping Work?

Track 3: Section #3 Introduction: Basic Necessary Equipment

Track 4: A Strong Voice

Track 5: A Flexible Voice

Track 6: A Dependable Voice

Track 7: The Demo

Track 8: Training

Track 9: Looping

Track 10: Section #4 Introduction: Basic Exercises

Track 11: Placement

Track 12: Attitude

Track 13: Age

Track 14: Dialect

Track 15: Rhythm

CD #2

Track 1: Social Level

Track 2: Celebrities

Track 3: Typical Animated Characters

Track 4: Section #5 Introduction: Is This for You?

Track 5: Voicing Inanimate Objects

Track 6: People Skills

Track 7: Reading Skills

Track 8: "C.I.A."

Track 9: Section #6 Introduction: Employment Opportunities in Cartoon/Character/Looping

Track 10: Character-Voice Work Outside of Cartoons

Track 11: Section #7 Introduction: How to Market Yourself

Track 12: Marketing After You Get the Job

Track 13: Write Your Own Commercial

Track 14: Analyzing Copy

Track 15: In Conclusion

Exercise Manual

Breath Control and Flexibility Exercise

CD 1, Track 5

Girl (In your highest possible pitch)

Villain (In your lowest possible pitch)

Hero (In your own beautiful voice)

Villain: You must pay the rent.

Girl: I can't pay the rent.

Villain: You must pay the rent!

Girl: But I can't pay the rent!

Hero: I'll pay the rent.

Girl: My hero.

Villain: Curses ... foiled again.

NOTES:

Placement Exercise

This is my head voice.

This is my nasal voice.

This is my adenoidal voice.

This is my throat voice.

This is my chest voice.

NOTES:

Some Favorite Tongue Twisters

1) Peter Piper picked a peck of pickled peppers. A peck of pickled peppers Peter Piper picked. If Peter Piper picked a peck of pickled peppers, how many pickled peppers did Peter Piper pick?

2) She sells seashells by the seashore. (*Repeat*)

3) Red leather, yellow leather, red leather, yellow leather. (*Repeat*)

4) Theopholis Thistle, the thrifty thistle sifter, in sifting a sieve full of unsifted thistles, thrust thrice three thousand thistles through the thick of his thumb. If Theopholis Thistle, the thrifty thistle sifter, in sifting a sieve full of unsifted thistles, thrust thrice three thousand thistles through the thick of his thumb, wouldst not thou, an unsuccessful thistle sifter, in sifting a sieve full of unsifted thistles, thrust more than thrice three thousand thistles through the thick of thy thumb? Success to the successful thistle sifter.

5) Said Ezra Pringle, English cleric, "Never enter an inn wherein winsome women wearing feathered finery sit waiting to tempt the timid and intemperate into sin. Let any man enter any such inn and he may never enter into heaven."

6) Red and yellow rubber baby buggy bumpers. (*Repeat*)

7) Ninety-nine nuns in an Indiana nunnery. (*Repeat*)

8) Betsy Botsom bought some butter, but she said, "This butter's bitter. If I put this bitter butter in the batter, it will make the batter bitter." So she bought some other butter, better than the bitter butter, and it made the batter better.

NOTES:

_____

_____

_____

_____

_____

_____

_____

_____

_____

_____

_____

_____

_____

_____

_____

_____

_____

_____

_____

_____

_____

_____

_____

_____

Dialect Exercise

Upscale British: I'm terribly sorry. What did you say? It seems the explosion has impaired my hearing. Have you a glass of brandy?

Ah-emm tedihbleh sod-ee. Wot deed you seh? Eat seems the exploesion has impaahed my hehding. Hev you a glahss uv brandih?

Cockney: What's that governor? You say your hearing is shot because of a bomb? Sorry, no liquor here.

Wuzzat guvneh? Yah sigh yaw earrin' is shoht cuz uvah bawm? Saw-ree, nou licker eah.

German: I was driving along the autobahn in my Volkswagen, when who should appear but the Gestapo!

I vass drrrivink alonk de owttobahn een mine Folksvahkun, ven who shuht appeah but de Geshtahpo!

Japanese: So sorry! I was educated in an American school, so my computer skill is terrible.

So sodhy! I wass edyou-kaytit een ahn Amedhican schoodh, so my computah skeedh iss tedheebudh.

Italian: My son is dead. <u>Your</u> son is dead. Pretty soon we're going to have no one to take over the family, eh?

Mah sone eesa det-ah. <u>You</u> sone eesa det-ah. Preety soon-ah we gonna have-ah no one-ah take ovah duh fahmilee, eh?

French: People ask, "(Gigi/Maurice), how can I be a great chef like you?" Ah. There is no way.

Pipple esk, "(Jhih-jhih / Mau-rrreese), ow ken ah be uh guh-rrrate chef lak yue?" Ah. Zehr iss noh weh.

NOTES:

_____

_____

_____

_____

_____

_____

_____

_____

_____

_____

_____

_____

_____

_____

_____

_____

_____

_____

_____

_____

_____

_____

_____

_____

_____

Hollywood Slavic

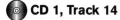

1) A recent immigrant — timid and hungry.
2) A deli owner — aggressive and self-important.

1) F. U. N. E. M.?

2) S., V. F. M.

1) F. U. N. E. X.?

2) S., V. F. X.

1) O. K., I. F. M. N. X.!

NOTES:

Cartoon/Character Voice Analysis Exercise

Name of Character _____

Is this a Primary Voice? _____

If "No," what is? _____

Attitude _____

Placement _____

Age/Energy _____

Texture _____

Rhythm _____

Fluctuation _____

Dialect/Regionalism _____

Social Class _____

Specialty _____

Personality Phrase _____

NOTES:

_____

_____

_____

_____

_____

_____

_____

_____

_____

NOTES:

Typical Animated Characters

Teen Hero/Heroine: Stay right where you are, Lord Zaydarr! Those crystals you stole from the Sky Palace belong to Princess Sheena. And I'm going to see that she gets them back!

Professor: That's right Chris. By modulating the frequency of the matter/anti-matter replicator, I've managed to buy us enough time to ... oh no ... Chris ... look out!

Villain: You're too late, Simpkins. I've already contacted your parents. They're on their way here even as we speak. Oh, and Simpkins? You can forget about the python you put in Miss Pillson's podium. It's been placed in the pokey!

Bimbo/Thug: Hey, Knuckles! Get a load of this! Lefty has developed a soft spot for some high society dame! Ha!

Alien: Foolish earthlings. Don't you understand that we can destroy your planet in the wink of an eye? No, huh? Oh. (What do we do now Glork? It doesn't cover any of this in the manual!)

Cute Creature: Hi! My name is Perky the Pea. All of us here in the pod are just green with envy over corn's popularity. We know you'd like us if you tried us, so all we are saying, is give peas a chance.

NOTES:

"Feathered Friends"

Grandma Duck: Yes! *(intoning)* When you care you want to share!

Duckling: No share! <u>MY</u> lily pad!

The other ducklings want to start the game. They start flapping,
so that their lily pads move like bumper cars.

Grandma Duck: It's time to start the game! Duckling and Baby Chick — you be <u>IT</u>!

BABY CHICK *starts to flap excitedly.*

Baby Chick: Share!

In flapping, she once again accidentally touches DUCKLING'S *hat.*
He stops flapping and turns on her.

Duckling: <u>MY</u> hat!

BABY CHICK, *momentarily intimidated, stops flapping.*

Baby Chick: Share?

Duckling: No share! <u>MY</u> hat! <u>MY</u> lily pad! <u>NO SHARE</u>!

NOTES:

Versatility Exercise

Please read each "dwarf's" name in a way that fits his/her personality.

I'm Happy

I'm Bashful

I'm Grumpy

I'm Dopey

I'm Sleazy

I'm Sweety

I'm Sneaky

I'm Angry

I'm Sexy

I'm Nutty

... and I'm Baby!

NOTES:

"Ode to Prescription Medicine"

Zit: Hey! We're those nasty pimples that trash your complexion. Look in the mirror!

Kid: Oh no, like, more zits. This is so bogus!

Zit: Hey! Cut that out! You squeeze me again and I'm gonna turn you into a pizza-face!

Kid: Mom! (Dad!)

Mom/Dad: Now honey (son), I've told you – all of us here in _____
(use a small town name appropriate to a regional dialect of your choice) know those drugstore medications are only for a simple pimple. Let's call the dermatologist.

Zit: Hey guys, she's (he's) callin' the derm! We're history!

Announcer: When your pimples get tough, don't fool around. See a dermatologist. This message brought to you by Leslie-Lake Laboratories.

NOTES:

Character-Voice

CD 2, Track 14

A. **Chuckles** *(talking through giggles):*

Chuckles. The fun cookie from Yumm-o. Two fun cremes in every cookie — fudge and vanilla. Free fun prizes in every box. Fun faces on every cookie. Available in chocolate and vanilla sandwich varieties. Chuckles. New from Yumm-o.

B. **Regal Crown Cola** *(quirky, laid-back, tongue-in-cheek):*

A contemporary love story from the makers of Regal Crown Cola:

Jack and Jill went up the hill. To fetch a pail of water. Jack fell down, and broke his Regal Crown. And Jill is now dating a guy from L.A.!

C. **Spud Skins** *(enthusiastic cowboy/cowgirl):*

Yeehaw! Kimmler introduces barbeque flavor Spud Skins. Doggone great barbecue taste and the a-peelin' flavor of baked potato skins. Makes 'em tangy little snackin' buddies. So get 'em, partner. They're new from Kimmler.

D. **Air Shamrock** *(warm, Irish, mystical):*

Greet the Irish morning from your room in an Irish castle. When you come to Ireland, you don't just look at our castles, you stay in 'em. See your travel agent or call Air Shamrock. Ireland — the unexpected pleasures.

CD 2, Track 14

"EASY-TUMM"

You're the voice of someone's stomach — unhappy at first and then hopeful.

Stomach: Hey. I'm your stomach. Listen, you know the heartburn that wakes us up at night? I think we might have erosive acid reflux disease. Ask the doctor about this new Easy-Tumm. Every stomach on the block is talking about it.

Announcer: TBD (**To Be De**termined)

Stomach: *(on hearing announcer talk about Easy-Tumm)* Heal? Did someone say heal? I love the sound of that word! I hear Easy-Tumm can cost up to a dollar less per day than the other prescription medicines for the same condition.

SFX: *(sounds of couple getting amorous)*

Stomach: That'll help us sleep better, too.

NOTES:

Character-Voice Script #3

CD 2, Track 14

"MAGIC TALKING MIRROR"

1) What shall we play today?

2) What shall we wear today?

3) Let's go shopping.

4) We're going to a party!

5) Let's brush my hair.

6) Let's go to the park.

7) It's time for a snack.

8) Let's tidy up my room! (For Moms — note the appeal.)

9) Let's brush my teeth!

10) I'm sleepy — it's time for bed (yawn).

NOTES:

Character-Voice Script #4

"CABLE-FILM"

Perform every line in a different voice, appropriate to each celebrity.

1) Who's got the genius of Hoffman,
   The face of Roberts,
   The madness of Nicholson,
   The heat of Pfeiffer,
   The wit of Murphy,
   The body of Schwarzenegger.
   Who's got all this?
   Cable Film. Always the best.

2) Who has the tenacity of Tyson,
   The style of Sugar Ray,
   The heart of Hearns,
   The courage of Chavez,
   The fortitude of Foreman,
   The agility of Ali.
   Who has all that raw talent in one explosive package?
   Cable Film. Always the best.

NOTES:

Character-Voice Script #5

CD 2, Track 14

"NOTIAN'S QUEST"

This is an audition script for a Japanimation video. The lines are often out of sequence. Your character clues come from the way the lines are written. The style is very energetic.

Kellka *(female):* That's how I managed to get away from this Momacho character. But my ship got banged up in the process and crashed here. Meanwhile, I went to sleep in the rejuvenator capsule ... Do you understand? Well, anyway ... I myself don't see the big picture 'til I find Grandpa's Ono Stabilizer. I think we've come far enough. Besides, if I don't use Ono energy, they can't trace me. The Ono spells have faded ... And what brought you out to that valley? Tomorrow, I'll find a town and fetch some groceries.

Oochi *(male/female):* Sir, we've arrived. Prepare for descent. Right away, Sir Momacho! Oochi # 5, 6, 7, 8, 9, follow the lead of #12 and proceed to the target site! Roger! Judging from the decay, I gather the ship crashed just after it disappeared from our monitoring system. I'm certain it came from here. I can see where the anti-Ono was penetrated.

Momacho *(male):* What a wasteland ... A fringe existence, indeed. What do I care? Just get us to the target, you useless cretins! Kellka, I can't wait to possess you ... and to have you show me a power that surpasses Diamond Thought. You hold the secret, Kellka! There's no way he's that powerful! He's backed up by Kellka or her ship! Maybe our ship malfunctioned. Dumb luck! A coincidence! We've got 10 more combatants! They couldn't possibly beat them all! My victory is guaranteed.

Notian *(male/female):* I was asked to protect her. She got married. She asked me to protect Mun for her. Don't cry. Help each other in need. It's the law of the desert. Once she got real mad and froze motion. Not too many people are as powerful as Mun. But most people have *some* power. I'll get them. I will protect you. That was the promise. Mun, are you okay? I will protect Kellka. I promised.

NOTES:

Character-Voice Script #6

CD 2, Track 14

"FLASH"

Guy or Gal with regional accent: Well, on one hand, I'm busy because I own my own restaurant — Mimi's (Jake's) on Route 57 North — open seven days a week. And I don't have time to wait around doing laundry. But on the other hand, I can't help it, I care about getting stuff clean. (Thank you very much, Mother.) Flash gets my entire wash clean — the way I want it — the very first time, every time. Now if I could just get my bookkeeper to come clean.

NOTES:

Character-Voice Script #7

CD 2, Track 14

"PINKY PLOTOPLASM"

The narrator is Pinky Protoplasm, a tiny, androgynous, adorable creature with a funny voice, designed to jazz up dry copy. If medical narration interests you, then you'll probably want to invest in a medical dictionary.

Pinky: The rheumatoid arthritis cell, the ragocyte, is a neutrophil in the synovial fluid, whose cytoplasmic vacuoles contain immunoglobulin and rheumatoid factor. Lysosomal enzymes, such as collagenase, elastase and cathepsins, are released from these neutrophils, or ragocytes, during phagocytosis, resulting in significant potential cartilage destruction.

NOTES:

Character-Voice Script #8

"PEARL PERIL"

Highly dramatic, lush and seductive.

Black Magic, a necklace worth a small fortune, has disappeared.

It <u>was</u> to be her financial security. Now, her only hope to get the pearls back is to team up with Lance Cameron, a man who might help her...if the price is right.

Pearl Peril.

Another book featuring the Cameron family, by best-selling author Janet Fowler.

Pearl Peril.

A race through uncharted waters that leads to adventure and romance.

Now available in paperback from Markum Books.

NOTES:

"Wandering Wireless"

CD 2, Track 15

Marilyn: With Wandering Wireless, I can do it anywhere.

Bogart: Sweetheart, can you do it in a car?

K. Hepburn: Of course, but I'd rather do it in a bar.

Mr. Fargo: Hon, can you do it in the snow?

Ms. Fargo: You betcha! I can do it all over Fargo.

Thug: Can you do it moving a piano?

Bimbo: Yeah! I can do it with Tony Soprano.

Mr. Southern: Darlin', can you do it on a farm?

Ms. Southern: Bubba, I can do it with one arm.

Mr. Japan: So sorry! Can you do it on a choo-choo train?

Ms. Japan: Hi! I can do it on a plane to Spain.

Mr. Scots: Can you do it while pushing a cart?

Ms. Scots: Aye laddie! I can do it while watching *Braveheart*.

Surfer Dude: Yo! Can you like do it wearing socks?

Valley Girl: Dude! I can, like, do it in detox.

Boris: Can you do it in the Kremlin?

Natasha: Boris, I can do it with Moose and Squirrel in the backseat of a Gremlin.

Sir Brit: Your Majesty, can you do it in the rain?

Q.E. II: I can do it while my son Charles <u>waits</u> to reign.

J. F. K.: Ask what you can do with your wireless. Can you do it in the air?

Marilyn: Oh yes, Mr. President. With Wandering Wireless, I can do it anywhere.

NOTES:

_____
_____
_____
_____
_____
_____
_____
_____
_____
_____
_____
_____
_____

_____

Audition /
Session Supplies

Recommended:

- Your demo, voice-over bio, business card (and any P.R. materials that you may have)
- Cell phone/pager
- Appointment/address book
- Pencils with erasers
- Passport and/or driver's license (picture I.D.)
- Your Social Security number/ your agent's phone number and address
- Your personal log to record pertinent information
- W-4 form, pre-filled out with all your personal tax details
- Area map
- Money for unexpected transportation requirements
- Bottle of water
- "Noisy items" pouch to store change/jewelry/keys prior to recording
- Breathspray/mints

Discretionary:

- Reading glasses
- Saliva substitute
- Lip balm
- Throat lozenges
- Hi-lighter (for *bookings* — mark *audition* copy in pencil only)
- Stopwatch
- Invoice book
- Portable tape player (and earphones) with tapes pertinent to the audition/job (includes dialect tapes, recorded celebrities, and "mood" music)
- Headshot/resume (if you also do on-camera)

Professional Tips

- It's imperative that you have a working, dependable voicemail number. Check your messages frequently, and return calls promptly.

- Carry a pager and/or cell phone (and turn it off during sessions; it can blow a take). If you must return a cell phone call, leave the room or speak very quietly; it's rude to assume that anyone is interested in hearing about your personal life.

- Make sure you have easy access to a fax machine. When booked on a long narration job, getting a fax copy in advance will give you time to do necessary research.

- Don't bring children or pets to an audition/booking. Rarely, a regular employer with whom you have a friendly relationship may ask to see the new baby, puppy, etc., but make sure you clear it first.

- Always be prompt, and 10 minutes early for an audition, 20 for a booking, is even better. (If you show up at an audition *extremely* early, you may be in the way.) You'll want time to settle down, sign in, study the copy, and have a drink of water. If the spot is a double, you'll want time to rehearse with your partner. "Shot out of a cannon" is never a good approach to performing, so allow for traffic problems, security check-ins, broken elevators, etc. If lateness is unavoidable, call in with an honest arrival time; they may tell you not to bother and you'll have to live with that disappointment, but they'll appreciate the information. You've heard, "time is money"? Well, studio time is *big* money; be respectful of that fact.

▸ Be prepared for overtime. Don't schedule your life so tightly that there's no room for flexibility. Auditions often run long, and if a producer at a booking says, "We want to try something else; can you stay?" the correct answer isn't, "No." Check your voicemail frequently after a session in case they need you to dash back to the studio to do a pick-up. Remember who's in power; you're there to serve.

▸ Be patient and courteous; no "attitude" or "spoiled diva" behavior allowed. Don't talk loudly in the audition's waiting area; walls are thin and you could blow someone's take. Don't hog the refreshments, public phone, or bathroom. At an audition, mark your script in pencil only; others also have to use it.

▸ The only acceptable attitude for a professional performer is *positive*. Anything negative is inappropriate. The voice-over world is a very small one, and any whining, nagging or begging will get you a "bad rep" in a heartbeat. Remember that your audition begins the minute you enter the building; be respectful and pleasant to everyone, starting with the doorman, and word will soon get around the business what a pro you are.

▸ Don't socialize too much before an audition; it wastes your prep time. Be friendly and pleasant, but remember that you're in competition with others for a job. Your fellow actors may be extremely generous or adept at sabotage, so protect yourself: focus and stay professional. Once you're in a session, take your cue from the clients; be ready to chat or ready to plunge into work, depending on the signals they give.

▸ Warm up privately. People aren't interested in how you get there, they just want to hear the results.

▸ Stay lubricated, but be careful with liquids around expensive sound equipment. Always ask if you may have your water in the booth, and where you may place it.

▸ Don't wear noisy clothes, such as squeaky leather or rustling nylon, to a sound session; remove jingling change, jewelry and keys before beginning to record.

▸ Watch your mouth. Mics are almost always "hot" (live), so even if none of those people on the other side of the glass seem to be paying any attention to you, they can probably hear every word you say. Negative comments and foul language are unprofessional.

▸ Take the time to assemble the "Audition/Session Supplies" listed in this book. Have your voice-over kit ready to go; if you wait until you're dashing out the door to that last-minute audition, you'll probably forget something.

▸ Adjust your copy stand (podium) so your copy is as level with your mouth as possible. If the copy is *too low*, your voice is going down to the page, rather than into the mic; stretching your neck up and reading *too high* into the mic constricts your throat. Folding the top (blank) portion of your copy page over the stand can stabilize it and bring it to a better reading level for you.

▸ Ask your partner in a double to rehearse; the worst he/she can do is refuse. (See "Fresh" in the *List of Terms* in this book.) Be prepared to switch roles in a double or multiple.

▸ Write thank-you notes. If you appreciated the helpful casting director, encouraging agent, and supportive engineer, let them know it. Everyone likes to be acknowledged.

▸ Read magazine ads and watch commercials; this is your marketplace and you need to be aware of changing trends. We could all learn from our technical friends: Just a few years ago, many recording studio engineers were using razor blades to edit reels of tape. They've since had to completely re-learn their craft to keep up with the new "computer-literate, digital, high-tech" world of sound. You, the voice talent, must be equally flexible in order to remain competitive.

▸ Be extremely careful about personal hygiene. A recording studio booth is a very small space, often shared with others for long periods of time. Bathe, wash your hair, and brush your teeth *often*. Make sure your clothes and your nails are clean. Don't smoke, because your skin and clothes absorb the odor; you probably can't smell it, but the rest of us only wish we couldn't. Be generous with deodorant application; be conservative in your use of cologne. Don't eat right before a session and neglect to brush your teeth; you might spray food residue on the mic, or on your fellow actors. (And imagine the reaction from the clients if you smile at them with food in your teeth.) If all this seems like overkill, so be it; I recommend that you err on the side of compulsive cleanliness rather than risk getting a reputation as a piggy actor with whom no one wants to share a booth. It's only polite to make sure you're not offensive, and it's part of being a professional.

▸ Giving a good level (see "Level" in the *List of Terms*) and a good slate (see "Slate") is imperative. Technique and terminology concerning studio procedures such as these can be acquired in a basic skills voice-over class.

▸ As a general rule, stand up to record spots and sit for narrations; but be prepared to stand if sitting isn't offered, and vice versa.

▸ Don't give unsolicited advice to your fellow actors; you may intend to be helpful, but it can come across as patronizing. Voice-over etiquette requires that you treat all other performers as equals.

▸ Don't try to memorize a line and raise your eyes off the page to say it; that's a very effective stage-actor technique, but voice-over actors stay "on" the copy. If you raise and lower your head as you speak, you'll change the sound level that your engineer has so carefully set. Aim for consistency.

▸ If left alone in the booth for long periods of time while discussions you can't hear are going on in the control room, don't get paranoid; they probably aren't even talking about you. Use the time to rehearse; it will keep your focus on the copy, where it belongs.

▸ Experiment with timing; get a stop watch and practice at home, so that when they say "Take two seconds off this 60-second read," you'll know what that feels like. You can practice with magazine ad copy, which is often written very much like a commercial.

▶ Don't tap or blow on the mic; it's a sure sign of an amateur. Don't cough, sneeze, or clear your throat directly into the mic, and always give warning before making shrill or high-volume sounds. The studio is filled with expensive, delicate equipment (and that includes your engineer's ears!).

▶ Don't stop a take, no matter how bad you think it is; it's not your responsibility. The engineer may be able to salvage something from an imperfect take for "cut & paste" purposes.

▶ Once the engineer has set your mic, don't change your position or you'll be "off-mic." Don't adjust your own mic; that's the engineer's job. Your job is acting: *specialize*.

▶ It's normal to feel nervous at a session; that's just your adrenaline kicking in, and it's not a serious problem as long as you're in control and don't start rushing. Deep, steady yoga breathing can be calming and increases oxygen, that natural mood elevator. Your breath control is an important tool in your voice-over equipment.

▶ Ask for, and be open to, feedback; even if it's negative. How else will you learn what's working? A desire for improvement, coupled with a thick skin, is an empowering combination.

▶ One of the reasons you get to a session early is so that you can check out your copy for unknown terms and pronunciations. Ask *before* you start the read and don't worry about appearing ignorant; it's often a preference issue, such as, "About 'data,' do you prefer 'dat-tah' or 'day-tah'?" The casting director/client will be glad you want to get it right; it shows professional concern. Sometimes you get no warning about unusual terminology. Early in my career, for example, I was doing a TV voice-over when the engineer directed me to "Bag the third graph, we'll catch it on chyron." Fortunately, the blank look on my face let my fellow actor in the booth know that I had no clue what that meant, so he took pity on me, went off-mic, and quietly informed me that it meant I should not read the third paragraph of the copy because those words would be seen as text on the TV screen. (The "chyron" technique is often used to showcase a company's trademark "tag.") If another actor doesn't translate for you, *ask*; "faking it" can get you in trouble. Of course, if you continue to study your craft, as you should, you'll pick up a lot of industry terminology along the way.

▸ Do your research prior to a session. The more preliminary work you do to become comfortable with the script, the more expensive studio time you'll save; another way to become known as a "cost-effective" actor.

▸ If you're asked to "overnight" your demo to a client, politely request the client's package-shipping company's account number; there's no reason you should have to pay for this potential employer's need-for-speed. Many people are now using computer "files" to send sound information quickly from one computer to another; you may want to offer this option to the client. I have my vocal samples on my website (www.talkingfunnyformoney.com) so clients can click on them and hear me immediately.

▸ If the client says, "Do it more like the second take," but you can't remember how you sounded way back then, politely ask for a "playback" of your read. In fact, (judiciously) requesting playbacks can be an excellent way to hear just what it is they want to adjust, when they're having no luck describing it.

▸ If, *after* giving casting directors/clients what they've requested, you want to offer a different approach to the character, politely ask, "May I try something?" (If you offer, make sure it *is* something different from what they've already heard.) Sometimes you'll begin a session with very little direction; you might hear, "What's your take on this?" The director may be honestly open to your ideas, or may have no clue what to do with this copy, or may just be lazy; whatever the reason, use it as an opportunity to demonstrate your creativity and command of your instrument. Your ability to analyze copy, and self-direct, can save a commercial that no one else could bring to life.

▸ At the end of a session, ask for business cards. Most people want to give them out; that's why they have them. You can get information for your mailing list from the cards, and once you've asked for them, it's perfectly acceptable to offer yours. (Offering yours first can make you seem a bit "pushy actor.")

▸ Keep your script after a booking; it's an addition to your practice file, and if you get called back for a pick-up, you can use it to refresh your memory of the spot. If it was a non-union job, having a copy of the script can aid in payment; along with your invoice, it proves you were there.

▸ Speaking of invoices, if you're doing non-union work, purchase an invoice book with self-carbons from the office supply store and carry it in your voice-over kit. Make sure you get the producer to sign your invoice at the end of the session, and

keep a copy for your records. You can create your own in\
using the standard form as a model, but don't forget to keep ،
signed copy, and make sure you've both given and gotten
enough information to get paid. Aside from the usual mailing
address, job description and amount due, you'll want to
include your Social Security number (they may be sending you
a 1099 for your taxes), and anything special, such as a job
number, that expedites your check. Have your invoice filled
out as completely as possible before the session; that way
you're not taking up valuable studio time doing paperwork.
(They want you out of there so that they can get on with "post-
production.") The same holds true for union jobs; you won't
present an invoice, but there will be other forms, such as con-
tracts, to sign. Ask your agent what to expect, so that you can
do the necessary paperwork as quickly as possible, say your
good-byes, and leave them to "the mix."

▸ Keep good records. Whether you've got an agent or not, you're
still the C.E.O. of your voice-over business, and if you get
audited, the I.R.S. probably won't respond very well to "Ask
my agent." Over the years, having an experienced tax pre-
parer, accountant, and financial adviser has saved me a great
deal of money (not to mention time and brain cells), but the
more organized I am, the less I have to pay them just for
straightening out my records. Also, like any business man-
ager, you need to be conscientious about saving and
investing. That unattractive "desperate actor" aura often
comes from living too close to the financial edge. Remember:
we're striving for "confident relaxation."

▸ Before you leave a session, express your delight with the material, and ask the powers-that-be for a copy ("dub," "dupe") of

ished product. They'll probably be flattered. Since the
asn't been mixed yet, the engineer will have to mail it to
he client has to approve this, but if present, can do so on
ot; much easier than trying to track him/her down later.
Always politely offer to pay for the dupe, though you probably
won't have to. I think a CD copy is best, because you can listen
to it at home and it's of high enough quality to be used for
editing onto your demo; but if all they'll send is a cassette,
pray it's a clear one. I ask for a copy of each spot I do, because
I never know what might be usable for future demo updates.

▸ Don't ignore the left side of TV ad copy where the visuals are
described. They can help you discover the overall mood of the
spot, and provide clues for your line readings.

▸ Keep a log of all classes, auditions, jobs, etc.: who you met,
how you felt, and what you learned. It will help you to track
your personal progress, and is a great aid for networking/mar-
keting. The best time to record this information is immediately
following the event, when it's fresh in your mind, and you have
access to practical information such as addresses and phone
numbers. The best marketers I know realize what a "personality profession" this is; they use their journals to remind them
of agents' birthdays, clients' favorite sports teams, and engineers' alma maters, knowing that taking a personal interest
sets them apart from the talent herd and makes them memorable. Speaking of memorable: *Remember all names.*

▸ Prior to a booking: plan your commute, get lots of sleep the
night before, and dress as you wish to be viewed. At the
booking, announce yourself to the receptionist and work on
your copy until they're ready for you. Don't have any dairy or
caffeine right before the job; dairy can increase mucus and

caffeine can make you hyper and dry out your throat. Keep those pipes clear!

▸ Smile as you enter a session, smile as you leave, and remember to smile during the recording when you say the name of the product; that puts "smile" in your voice.

▸ Don't buy into the old actor complaint of "Oh, business is so slow." (Or "seasonal," or "cyclical," or whatever the current excuse is for a lack of activity.) My biggest job *ever* happened one July (in the supposedly "dead" summer months), because I hustle *every day*. If there are no actual bookings or auditions, use the "down time" to study, organize your marketing materials (organize your *life*), exercise, work more hours at your survival job (to save money for career investment, right?), or learn a language. Speaking of being bi-lingual, if you're already close, acquiring fluency can be a smart career move, as there's lots of "language" work in the voice-over world. Anything you do that's creative feeds your soul and enhances your artistry, so put your free time to good use and paint, write, dance, volunteer, *whatever*; anything but "wait by the phone." (That's self-destructive, non-productive, "desperate actor" behavior.)

▸ When you're reading copy, start and finish clean; don't "drift in and drift out," as that indicates a lack of commitment to your material and your character.

▸ Be prepared for a client to say, "Tell me a little about yourself." This is a method used to get you to loosen up and show the personality that might contribute to making a unique spot. If given this opening, don't just recite your credits! Practice interesting, appropriate smalltalk with your fellow actors and friends, so you'll be ready if given the chance to be "spontaneous."

▸ If you're a beginner, inexpensive introductory voice-over classes can often be found at local colleges and vocational schools, but whatever level you're on, you should continue to study, study, study (particularly with industry professionals who can recommend you!). To further your career, you need practice and exposure: *Practice* because skills-enhancement gives you a competitive edge, and *exposure* because work breeds work. So: use your voice in any way you can. Focus on classes where you *talk*; oral interpretation and public speaking courses are usually readily available, and will help you get rid of any "nerves" you might have. Do poetry readings. Volunteer to do "new play" readings. Let casting directors know you're eager to volunteer as a "reader" for auditions. (If you *do* work as a reader, remember that you're there to showcase the auditioner; but giving a professional, well-acted read could lead to you being considered for a future job.) Participate in "open-mic" night at comedy clubs. Become a storyreader at your local library, hospital, or senior citizens' residence; many of my colleagues volunteer as radio-readers for the blind. (This is really trial-by-fire; there you are, broadcasting on the air, *ice cold*!) Try to get in plays, unpaid venues or not. Many community-service and religious organizations sponsor theatre groups that are (relatively) less competitive than Off Broadway; any acting you do will inform your voice-over work, and there's always the chance that some ad agency executive could see you in a play and decide that your voice is perfect for a client's upcoming campaign. (Happened to me.) Take any class at all about the commercial world you're entering, not just those about performing — understanding copywriting, how ad agencies operate, the workings of a recording studio — can give you great insight into those folks "on the other side of the glass." Volunteer to be a "go-fer" for the sound person on an independent or student film: you'll absorb lots of terminology, and meet people (remember *networking*?), who share your interest in the entertainment industry.

▸ We all have friends in the corporate world; convince a business acquaintance to try a radio ad with you as the talent. If you're union, you can offer to work for scale; if you're not union, you can offer to work for a reasonable fee. Do the legwork so that you can present all the facts and figures, and make it easy for this potential employer to take a chance. Radio is relatively inexpensive, but it's a foreign advertising medium to many corporations, so if you can make apparent its revenue-enhancing potential, you might just create a voice-over job for yourself. The experience and exposure will be worth the effort.

▸ Don't price yourself out of the market. (To know typical salaries, you must study the local market trends.) Know, and take pride in, your worth, but don't underestimate the "value of volume." That means lots of low-paying, non-glamorous jobs may get you better exposure than one big one; remember, every time you're in front of a mic, your voice-over network expands. I know that one of the reasons I've gotten a lot of voice-over jobs over the years is the simple fact that I have no problem working for "scale," meaning the lowest fee the client is allowed by union rule to pay me. Insulting? Doesn't bother my ego at all, because ego is one of those luxuries (along with attitude), that I never bothered to acquire: they're both counter-productive. The operative word in the phrase "becoming and remaining a working actor" is *working* — as often and as well as you can.

▸ Analyze your desire to be a voice-over actor, and know why you're doing this; having a clear motivation will help you through the tough times. If you're performing for some less-than-healthy reason, you're probably wasting your time trying to have a voice-over career. Despite your best efforts to fake it, negative feelings will always show in your voice and prevent successful bookings, so if you're not having fun, do yourself a favor and get out of this very demanding business before you've spent any more time and money.

▸ If you fluff, let it go! Don't dwell on mistakes: apologize for them, learn from them and move on.

▸ Your only enemy is fear: it causes nervousness, which leads to self-sabotage. Do whatever it takes to get calm enough to listen. All your clues for success come from *listening*.

▸ A professional actor has professional behavior, skills and materials.

▸ In your voice-over work, always strive to sound like a person talking rather than an actor reading. "Talking" means "speaking thoughts." It's the first time you've had the thought that's written in the script, so it should sound as though it's the first time you've said it. Our recurrent goal is a fresh and believable read.

▸ Present yourself as you wish to be viewed: a full-time, professional, successful voice-over actor.

▸ In the voice-over world, as in life, *be prepared for anything!*

List of Terms

Accent 1. The stress you put on a syllable, word or phrase. **2.** Another word for dialect. I usually use "dialect" and save "accent" to refer to stress/emphasis.

Active Commercial The opposite of "passive commercial." See "Hard Sell."

Ad Agency A company that produces advertising for other companies; we're particularly interested in those that focus on "broadcast" or "on-air" commercials.

A.D.R. **A**utomated **D**ialogue **R**eplacement. (Sometimes referred to as **A**utomatic **D**ialogue **R**eplacement, and I've also heard **A**udio **D**irect **R**ecord.) Part of looping terminology. The sound editor in charge of looping is called the A.D.R. Editor, or simply "the A.D.R. "

A.F.T.R.A. **A**merican **F**ederation of **T**elevision and **R**adio **A**rtists. Usually written and pronounced, "AFTRA." A labor union for commercial/industrial talent; this performers' union normally covers jobs involving "tape" (including radio and the "soaps," or daytime dramas) while SAG covers film.

Agency Demo A demo, usually a CD, put out by a talent agency. It contains a short vocal sample of each of its signed actors. Sometimes called a "house demo" or "house reel." Some voice-over organizations also assemble these, and for a fee you can be included. A group CD can be a good promotional tool, as an organization might have more comprehensive client mailing lists than you do, but weigh the cost of being on the demo and investigate the number of other voice-over actors on it *with* you (and how similar they are to you in vocal type), before making your decision to participate.

Air If you pause too long between words or sentences, you've left too much "air."

Ambiance The background noise under a vocal track; also called a "bed." May be music, sound effects, or a combination of both.

Annc. Abbreviation for "announcer." You'll usually see it written this way on commercial copy.

Attitude 1. The emotional through-line that you give to the character you're playing in the script. (A positive thing.) **2.** In modern terminology, this word has become a shortened form of "*bad* attitude," referring to the "spoiled diva" approach to dealing with people. (Most definitely a negative thing!)

Audition A non-paid casting session. Several actors read for the same role to determine who the client wants for the job. (Sometimes the best actor actually gets it!)

Avail. Abbreviation for "availability." An agent might call and say "I'm checking your avail. for next Tuesday at 11 am." This is not a guarantee of work; don't get too excited until it's a "booking."

Bed See "Ambiance."

Be Real A phrase you might hear in an audition for a "soft sell" commercial.

Billboard To emphasize or vocally highlight a portion of the copy.

Board The recording studio's audio console, or control panel, which the engineer operates.

Booking A confirmed recording session. (Hooray, you got the job!)

Booth The part of the studio where the talent records the script; usually separated from the control room by glass.

Break See "Damaged."

Break Character To suddenly "drop" your character during a performance and begin to speak as yourself or another character. If it's due to a loss of concentration, it's a very negative thing; if it's done intentionally for comic effect, it can be positive.

Breathy A whispery vocal quality.

Bright A clear vocal quality that usually "cuts through" the ambiance of a spot. Opposite of "warm."

Bring It Up (Down) To raise (lower) volume and/or energy. (Make sure you're clear on which one they want!)

Bump A request for a grace period, as in "We need you for an hour with a half-hour bump." The extra time may not be necessary, but the client wants to build the possibility that it will be into the session.

Bumper The corporate sponsor's "funding for this program provided by" statement heard at the front and back (like the bumpers on a car) of a non-commercial program.

Buy As in, "It's a buy," meaning they like it.

Buy-Out A one-time-only fee that you get instead of residuals.

Cable Spot A commercial that runs on the cable channels.

Cadence The phrasing you use when reading copy.

Callback If you get a callback, you're being "called back" for a second audition. They've selected the actors they're most interested in (the "callback actors"), and will now choose one of them for the job. (Unless they decide to "go a completely different way"!)

Cans Another term for headphones. I've also heard the term "ears."

Casting Director The person who finds the talent for the job. He/she may ask agents for actor submissions, or call talent directly.

Cattle Call A casting session that appears to include every actor in town. When the client isn't specific, the casting director is sometimes forced to cover all bases.

Character The role you're playing. "Character work" in commercials generally means portraying broadly-drawn, often humorous entities known as "types."

Class A Spot What we aspire to. A commercial that runs during prime-time on one of the network channels. Residuals are highest for this type of spot.

Click A type of mouth noise.

Client The owner of the product to be advertised.

Cold Read A performance without any rehearsal.

Color It To add various aspects of personality or "life" to a read; to give differing shades of meaning.

Commit What you must do to give a believable performance. To "commit" to your character means you are fully focused and invested; willing to look like a fool and totally unconcerned about it.

Comml. Abbreviation for "commercial."

Conflict 1. An agent may decline to "sign" you because the agency already has a "signed" client with a similar sound to yours, and that would "represent a conflict." **2.** If you do two different commercials for the same type of product and your voice is recognizable, you are "in conflict." (And in big trouble.) Therefore, if you've done a spot for Pepsi using your own unique voice, and then Coke wants you, it's up to you to say, "I'm sorry, I have a conflict." Character voices aren't confronted with this problem very often, since we usually sound completely different on each job.

Console See "Board."

Control Room The part of the recording studio where the client, writer, producer, engineer, etc. (everyone except the talent), all work during a session. Usually separated from the booth by glass.

Copy Another word for script. The text of a spot or narration, which you read aloud.

Copy Points The important items in a script; the points that require particular attention from the voice talent. These are often in the form of adjectives. ("The *fastest* but *safest* car," for example.)

Corporate Voice-Over A non-broadcast recording, usually made for a corporation's employees' in-house use. Your fee will be a "buy-out." This type of job is also referred to as an "industrial."

Cue The audible or visual sign from your engineer that tells you when to begin reading your copy.

Cue Pick-Up If you're slow to start speaking after your partner in a double has finished, you have "slow cue pick-up." If your cue pick-up is too fast, you'll overlap the other actor's lines, also known as "jumping the cue," or "stepping on lines." We want to achieve "*perfect* cue pick-up." This comes from innate good timing (and lots of practice!).

Cut This means stop.

Cut & Paste To assemble a finished spot out of parts from many "takes." Today this is done on a computer, but the term is left over from the era when the splicing of tape was done manually using razor blades and adhesive tape.

Cuts Through When your voice cuts through, it can be heard easily through background music and sound effects. "Bright" voices generally "cut through" more readily than "warm" ones.

Cutting Edge Sometimes called "edgy." A term meaning modern, trendy, "now," as in "soft sell but with a charismatic, individual, off-beat delivery"!

Cycle Commercial usage is broken up into 13-week periods called "cycles." The more cycles the spot plays, the more residuals for you.

Damaged A term generally used to describe a voice with a husky, smoky, or textured quality; one with a "break" or "fracture" on certain tones. A "damaged" voice (as an industry term) can be a perfectly healthy one and very interesting to hear, but if you have a *truly* damaged voice from a medical, nicotine, caffeine, or controlled-substance problem, then you're not managing your instrument; it's managing you and limiting your casting potential.

DAT An acronym for **D**igital **A**udio **T**ape. A small tape cartridge onto which sound is recorded digitally.

Dead Air What is heard when your pause is too long.

Demo 1. An abbreviation of "demonstration," as in a tangible demonstration, or sample, of your vocal abilities. Your "demo" demonstrates your talent. **2.** A preliminary version of a spot that is used by an ad agency to sell a concept. (Sometimes the demo is so good, it's tidied up a bit and run as an actual spot. In that case, you should be paid a commercial rate rather than a demo rate.)

Dialogue 1. The words in the copy. **2.** When actors in a scene talk to each other it's a "dialogue," as opposed to one actor performing a "monologue."

Digital Recording To convert sound into a series of numbers that are stored on a computer's hard drive, on a DAT, or on a CD.

Director The person who is in charge during a recording session. If the session personnel consists only of you and the engineer, then the engineer is also your director. (If the engineer indicates that you are to direct yourself, be prepared to do so.)

Donut The type of spot that occurs when there is pre-recorded material at the beginning and end, with a "hole" left in the middle for your voice. The parts can also be reversed, with your voice surrounding pre-recorded material.

Double A two-person spot.

Drop To "drop" your volume or intensity means to lower it.

Dry Mouth A condition (caused by nerves, smoking, exhaustion or health problems) that can lead to the dreaded "mouth noise."

Dub 1. A copy; also called a "dupe" (short for "duplicate"). Beware of "dupe houses" (companies who make copies of your demo from your master), who work with "high-speed dubs," as opposed to "real-time dubs." High-speed saves them time, but sometimes the quality of your demo suffers. 2. To "dub" a foreign-speaking actor means that you will replace his/her language with English (working from a translated script that usually needs some tweaking to make it "sync").

Dupe See "Dub."

Echo A repeated sound. Not the same thing as "reverb," although the two words are often used synonymously.

Edgy As in "This voice is edgy;" has an "edge." See "Cutting Edge."

Edit To cut and rearrange selected audio components into the finished "take."

Ellipsis The three periods in a row that usually indicate a thoughtful pause. You've probably noticed them in ... oh, you know what I mean.

Engineer The person who operates all the equipment in the recording studio. Your new best friend.

Establish When you see "Establish music (or sound effects) then under" on a script, that means sound will begin the spot and then quickly drop in volume so that your voice can be heard.

E.Q. An abbreviation for "equalize." The engineer controls the bass and treble with an "equalizer," to make your voice "brighter" (with more treble) or "warmer" (with more bass).

Face Actor A performer who is seen on-camera. (As opposed to off-camera voice actors who are invisible and anonymous, and can play three-year-olds forever!)

Fade As in "fade-in" or "fade-out." Your engineer may technically fade in/fade out sound when required, but if your voice "fades in and out" because you're turning your head away from the mic and back again while speaking, then you've blown the take and wasted valuable studio time. (My advice: Stay on mic!)

False Start The term used when the talent makes a mistake or "fluff" during the first few lines of the read. The take is usually stopped (don't *you* stop; it's the engineer's decision), and you'll be instructed to either "go again right away" on the same "slate," or a new take will be slated.

Fix-In-The-Mix Mistakes that are not dealt with during the session must be corrected by the engineer in post-production, when he/she is "mixing" all the elements for the finished spot.

Fluctuation How much your voice goes up and down the scale as you speak. Most of us don't have much vocal fluctuation in our normal voices; we stay within a few notes. (This isn't true of our character voices, of course!)

Fluff A mistake in your read.

Foley Room The area where the sound effects for a film or commercial are created. Looping is often done here because the room is large enough to accommodate a big group of voice actors, but loopers need to remember that the room usually has a hollow bottom. (The floor gets lifted to access stairs, gravel pits, etc. used for sound effects), so any "foot noise" will be magnified and probably picked up by the mic.

Fracture See "Damaged."

Franchised Talent agents who have agreed to abide by the guidelines of the performers' unions are "franchised." A union actor's agent must be a franchised agent.

Freelance A term applied to an actor who hasn't signed a contract with a talent agency that states he/she will be represented exclusively by that agency. "Freelance" talent may be submitted for jobs by anyone (keeping in mind that if you're union, you must abide by union rules). *Any* talent, freelance or not, should constantly seek out work on his/her own. (Don't wait by the phone; take charge of your career!)

Fresh 1. "Keep it fresh" means "please sound as though this is the first time you've uttered these lines, even though this is take number 115." 2. You approach your fellow-actor, with whom you're about to audition for a "double," and ask to rehearse, but he/she says, "No thanks, I want to keep it 'fresh'." That means this actor doesn't want to rehearse. You can't force the issue, you can only focus on your own positive energy and technique, and do your best in the audition. Having said that, let me also say, I'm always amazed by people who give up any opportunity to rehearse before performing with a stranger! The chance to get used to each other's timing, to prepare special interactive vocal moments, to gain the trust of your fellow talent and get that wonderful feeling of confident relaxation: Who wouldn't want *that*?! I personally think the "I want to keep it fresh" people are either lazy, afraid you're going to steal their ideas, or devoid of the technique that allows them to learn from each "read," whether it be a rehearsal or a performance.

From Off This term means you're intentionally off-mic, so as to sound as though you're in another room, or area.

Gig Another word for job. You've "booked" a "gig"!

Good Pipes If you have "good pipes," you have a strong, flexible, dependable instrument.

Go Up For To be submitted for, and audition for, a job. (In theatre, to "go up" means that you've forgotten your lines; since we voice actors don't memorize, we are spared that embarrassment!)

Graph An abbreviation for "Paragraph."

Hard Sell The opposite of "soft sell." Sometimes called an "active commercial." This type of spot requires a high-energy, aggressive delivery; but we still smile and love the product!

Hold An agent may call and say you're "on hold" for the spot you just auditioned for; that means the client is interested, but it's not yet a booking. You can still get the dreaded call that says you've been "released from hold."

Holding Fee Once every 13-week cycle, for as long as the commercial is being "held" for broadcast by the ad agency, the talent receives a "holding fee."

Hook The moment in the copy that connects with the listeners. The thing that makes the audience continue to listen, remember the spot, and buy the product.

Hot Mic A microphone that is turned on. Also called a "live mic."

House Demo See "Agency Demo."

Industrial See "Corporate Voice-Over."

In-House A term meaning "within a company's own walls." A job is an "in-house production" when the firm has its own recording studio; if the work is produced outside, solely for the use of the company, it is to be "viewed in-house only."

Insert To put a short segment of lines into an existing script.

Insurance See "Safety."

In The Can Completed.

Invest See "Commit."

J-Card A paper label which is inserted into a clear plastic cassette box. It has a "J" shape when folded and viewed from the side, hence the name.

Laundry List A series of descriptive words in a script. (See "Copy Points.") As the talent, your objective is to sound as though you're *not* reciting a laundry list, but giving varying emphasis to each item in the series, and thereby investing the copy with variety and life.

Lay It Down A term meaning "record it."

Leader The blank tape at the beginning of a demo cassette. A leader that is unusually long may make clients think they're listening to the wrong (blank) side of the cassette.

Level This refers to how loudly or softly you read the script, and the energy you give it. At the beginning of a session, your engineer may say, "give me a level." It's important that you begin to read the copy exactly as though you had heard, "Take one." The engineer is setting his/her equipment according to your projection, so giving a token-energy read, or reciting, "Mary had a little lamb," will not serve either of you; the engineer needs to know whether to adjust the mic position, change filters, etc., to make you sound as good as possible. I always continue "giving a level" until instructed to stop; it's extra rehearsal/warm-up time for me.

Live Mic See "Hot Mic."

Looping Replacing a voice track when the original track is unusable. The voice talent watches a movie or commercial scene, then lip-syncs replacement dialogue into the face actor's mouth until the new soundtrack perfectly matches the picture. When looping a crowd scene, we don't lip-sync a specific actor, but instead record "wild" lines to be used at the A.D.R. editor's discretion.

Major Markets The three major voice-over markets are New York, Los Angeles and Chicago. There will usually be flashier jobs and more money in those cities, but excellent voice-over work can be done any-where. During my college years I had a thriving voice-over career in Richmond, Virginia; I learned from highly professional people and enjoyed every moment of it. (And sometimes it's nice to be a big fish in a small pond!)

Marking Giving less than 100% to your performance. There's no excuse; if you're that tired, you should go home and make room for the totally-committed actor the client deserves.

Master The original recording from which demo copies ("dubs," "dupes") are made. Keep your master in a safe place, and don't give it away as a demo by mistake!

Mic An abbreviation for microphone (also spelled "mike"). There are three main types you'll find in a recording studio: The *Cardioid* type picks up sound from a heart-shaped area in front of the mic, and enables the talent to make minor head movements without going "off-mic." The *Figure Eight* allows two people to face each other and speak while using the same mic. The *Omni-Directional* picks up sound from all sides of the mic. There are other types, such as the *Shotgun* and the *Boom*, but they're not as common in recording studios.

Mix The "mix" is achieved when all audio elements — music, sound effects and voice — are combined to create the final soundtrack.

Moment Before This refers to what was going on in your character's life right before starting to speak the lines in the script. If you're thinking about *that*, instead of "Please let me get this job," or "Please make them like me," it will help ground your performance in reality, give it life, and prevent "nerves." (I've also heard this called "pre-life.")

Monologue A script for one person. When you talk with another actor, you're having a "dialogue."

MOS Silent. Stands for "**M**it **O**ut **S**ound."

Mouth Noise The sounds caused by "dry mouth," dental appliances, and speech impediments. Chronic mouth noise means an engineer has to spend studio time removing sounds from the recording, and keeps you from being cost-effective. (Also called "clicks & pops.")

Moving Off If you see "moving off" written on your script as a line direction, speak as you walk away from the mic, but be careful of foot noise. Sometimes the booth is too small to actually go very far, so you have to compensate by lowering your volume while moving just your head off-mic. Your engineer will guide you.

Multiple A spot calling for more than two performers. (A three-person spot is often called a "triple.")

Narration A voice-over job with a long script. Since a "spot" is usually 60 seconds or under, "long" is a relative term; a narration may be one page, or months' worth of steady work. (A new and wonderful form of survival job!)

National An industry term meaning a spot that runs throughout the entire country. "National network" means the spot will run on the major network channels, hopefully during primetime. (That makes it a "Class A Spot," and you get to pay some bills!)

Off-Camera The "off-camera" talent is unseen, and supplies only the voice for a TV spot, film, or video.

On-Camera The "on-camera" talent is seen. This often pays more than voice-over work, but requires longer hours under hot lights.

One-On-One See "Soft Sell."

Over This means a spot has gone over its time limit; it's too long.

Overlapping If you start speaking before your fellow actor has finished his/her line, you're "overlapping." Rarely, you may be instructed to overlap in order to achieve a specific effect; if not intended, it indicates a lack of technique. (See "Cue Pick-Up.")

Over-Modulate To speak too loudly.

Over The Top Or "O.T.T." for short. This means your performance is coming across as too broad. (Since no read is too broad as long as it's based in the character's reality, and "filled" with your commitment and skills, you'll need to take a look at all those areas and decide which need work.) Even the most outrageous creature in the cartoon universe must be believable.

Paper Noise Sound created by your script; it can blow an otherwise usable take. If a script stand is provided for you, use it, and don't adjust your copy after you've arranged it on the stand. If the copy consists of two pages, place them side-by-side so that you can see them both. If it's a narration script of many pages, go through and mark "page turn" places where you can pause, make a lot of noise, and then cleanly return to your read, knowing that the engineer will edit out all that paper shuffling. If there's no script stand, hold your copy steady; no rattling.

Passive Commercial The opposite of "active commercial." See "Soft Sell."

Pause A sound delay. A voice-over pause is usually shorter than normal, so as not to create "dead air."

Paymaster A company hired by the producer to handle payroll for the project. When you realize that payment sometimes has to go from the client, to the union, to the paymaster, to the agent, before you get *your* share, that long wait for the check suddenly makes sense!

Personalize If you're instructed to "Personalize it," that means your read is too standard; they want to hear some of your own personality in your performance. (Make sure you only expose the *positive* aspects of your nature!) If your unique approach jives with how the client wants the product represented, you might just get the job over hundreds of others. (Remember the "fluke factor"?)

Phonemes The units of sound that make up words. For example: the "t" sound in "talk."

Pick It Up A direction meaning "read faster."

Pick-Up To perform an internal section of the script. If you hear, "We'll do a pick-up on the third line," it means they like the rest of your read, and will edit your newly-performed line into it.

Pitch How high or low your voice is.

Placement Where your sound is coming from. The five main placements in the *Talking Funny for Money* workshop are Head, Nasal, Adenoidal, Throat, and Chest.

Play Against Type To perform a standard character in a way that isn't typical. If you're playing "the Villain," and decide to give him the voice of Shirley Temple, you are *definitely* playing against type! When this approach works, it can lead to a unique and memorable portrayal, but always be prepared to offer the stereotype as well: what seemed so amusing to the casting director at the audition may scare the client at the actual booking.

Playback To hear what you just recorded.

Pop A mouth noise, usually from plosive "P's" and "B's."

Pop Filter A foam or fabric cover placed over a microphone to help prevent "pops." Sometimes called a "windscreen."

Post A shortened version of "post-production." All the work that's done after the talent leaves: editing, music selection, mixing, etc.

Producer The person in charge of organizing and budgeting the project. The producer may be on the phone during your entire recording session. Don't take it personally; coordinating all the many aspects of a production is a complicated and demanding task.

Promo An abbreviation for "promotional spot." It promotes an event, product or service, and usually invites the audience to watch or listen to something.

Protection See "Safety."

Pull Breaths To remove the sound of an actor's breathing from the recording. If, due to the length of a spot, you're forced to "grab air" quickly and the inhalation is audible, the engineer may "pull your breaths." This makes the spot shorter as well as more attractive. If your audible gasping is caused by something other than extreme time constraints, you'll need to address that problem in order to be competitive.

Push To force. Usually a negative comment about your read, as in, "You're pushing" (trying too hard: we see you working at it), or "Don't push" (don't hard-sell the product).

Range Your vocal parameters. Cartoon/character/looping voice-actors strive for the largest range possible, so as to offer variety to the client and be cost-effective, whereas a "Voice-of-God" announcer may have a range consisting of all of three notes, and make a fortune anyway!

Read You of course "read" a script, but in the voice-over world your "read" is your *delivery* of that script — your performance.

Read Against The Text To read a line with a non-standard delivery. See "Play Against Type."

Reel At one time, demos consisted of actual reels of tape (a "reel" problem to lug around and store, I can assure you!). For a while cassettes were the standard tool, and now CDs have taken over. Who knows what we'll be asked to invest in next? Whatever it is, you'll probably still occasionally hear, "Send me your reel," meaning your demo.

Residuals One of my favorite things in the whole wide world. Residuals are "re-use" payments to run a commercial; the longer the better! If the client decides, for whatever reason, not to "run" the commercial (that means broadcast it) after it's recorded, the talent receives nothing except the session fee. If it "runs" for years, then so do your residual payments.

Reverb An abbreviation for "reverberation." It's a quality of resonance that an engineer adds to your voice electronically. It can be subtle, or so extreme as to make you sound "other-worldly." See "Echo."

Romance The Copy To sound as though you've absolutely fallen in love with the product.

Roomtone The sound a room makes when no one is in it. Each room has a unique sound, so recording "pick-ups" in the same studio in which you did the original session can be a very important issue; the "pick-ups" must match the original recording's roomtone. If an A.D.R. editor in a looping session says, "give me roomtone," then sit there quietly and breathe.

Run-Through A rehearsal. (Don't blow it off; imagine they've just said, "Take one.")

SAG Stands for **S**creen **A**ctors **G**uild; usually written and pronounced "SAG." It's a labor union for film talent; that includes voice-over actors recording their voices onto film.

Safety You may be told, "Give me a safety." That means they like your read, and want to have an additional take just like it as a back-up. This is your chance to give another brilliant performance. Also called "protection" and "insurance."

S.A.S.E. Stands for **S**elf-**A**ddressed **S**tamped **E**nvelope. Many actors include these when mailing their demo/P.R. package, so the recipient can conveniently return it if not interested. Personally, I don't, because I want my demo "lying around the office" as long as possible; if they're not interested they can always throw it away. (The cost of the demo is a tax deduction for me.)

Scale The union-designated minimum salary for a specific project. A union actor is not allowed to work for less, but is allowed to work for more, i.e., "double scale," "triple scale," etc.

Script The written text for a performance.

Sell As in "hard sell/soft sell" or "less sell/more sell." This refers to how much you're pushing the listener to buy the product.

Session The event at which the talent performs and records the script of the production.

Session Fee The payment you receive for your performance at the recording session.

SFX An abbreviation for "sound effects." May also be written as "EFX" or "FX." "SFX" can also mean music; in any event, it doesn't refer to you, the voice actor, so if you see, "SFX: 'Hello'," *Don't* say "Hello," because it's been pre-recorded.

Shave It If an engineer says, "Shave it by two," he/she wants you to take, or "shave," two seconds off your read.

Sibilance An extreme "S" sound in your voice. If you have sibilance, due to a lisp, dental appliances, etc., you must address this issue in order to be competitive.

Signatory A producer who has signed the AFTRA and/or SAG union contract, and thereby agrees to observe union guidelines and rates.

Signature The elements of your voice that make it uniquely yours. No one sounds exactly like someone else, but recognizing a vocal "signature" can make an impersonation a great deal easier.

Signed If you're a "signed client" with a talent agency, that firm will provide exclusive representation for you. You're not allowed to be submitted for jobs by other agencies, but you may seek work on your own.

Single A one-person spot. The copy will be a "monologue."

Slate This is the audible announcement of the take number that is recorded before you read. During an audition, you will, or will not, be responsible for slating the take, according to the requirements of the casting director. During a session, it's rare that you will be giving a slate; the engineer will assume that responsibility.

Smile The quality in your voice that denotes approval of the product. If you physically smile when speaking, your read will have "smile."

Smoke A textured quality in your voice. See "Damaged."

Soft Sell The opposite of "hard sell." Also called a "passive commercial." You may be told, "It's one-on-one, so don't act, don't announce, don't sell, don't romance the copy, just be natural, be yourself and talk to me." (But remember, you're still there to promote the product!)

Spec An abbreviation for "speculative." This means your payment is postponed until the project sells; you're working "on spec."

Splice The point in the recording where two different audio elements are edited together. This is a term left over from the era of tape and razor blades, when the "splice" was physical; now the editing is done by computer.

Spokes An abbreviation for "spokesperson." A "spokes" voice is usually strong, confident, and authoritative — the very qualities that a client wants to represent the product. (Then again, a company with a parrot in its logo once hired me to voice its "spokes-parrot!")

Spot A radio or television commercial. In the days of live broadcasts, commercials were performed "on the spot between shows," hence the term. A TV spot is usually called a voice-over because it's a "voice over a picture."

Stairsteps A long list of adjectives in a spot, requiring increased energy on each one.

Station I.D. A short spot that announces the call letters of a radio or TV station.

Step On Lines See "Cue Pick-Up."

Storyboard An artist's rendering of a commercial. A storyboard is often posted at voice-over auditions so the talent can understand the visual aspects of the spot; this can aid in interpretation.

Studio An audio isolation room, usually divided by glass into the booth for the talent, and the control room for everyone else.

Submitted When an agent sends your name into the casting director as a potential auditioner, you're being "submitted" for the job.

Sync Short for "synchronize." To make simultaneous sounds. This word is often used in lieu of "lip-sync," meaning to replace sounds coming out of a face actor's mouth with new sounds, perfectly matched to the picture.

Tag A very short spot, or a short portion of a spot, usually placed at the end. This phrase is strongly identified with the product: "This Bud's for you," and "Did somebody say McDonalds?" are examples of well-established product tags. There are some voice actors who only do tags; someone else does the body of the spot at a different time. If the tag is a "live tag," the announcer — often a radio D.J. — supplies it live at the time of broadcast.

Take Every read of the copy is called a "take."

Talent The performer. (That's you!)

Talent Agent The person whose firm serves as an actor's representative in organizing auditions, scheduling bookings and negotiating payment. The agent receives a percentage of the actor's fee, and usually represents a pool of talent called "signed clients." Some agents also represent "freelance talent."

Talkback The audio system that permits the people in the control room to talk with the talent in the booth.

Test An unpolished version of a commercial made to "test" the market. If the test has a high approval rating, an actual spot may be warranted.

Texture See "Damaged."

Three Beeps The sound cue system used to let a loop-actor know it's time to talk.

Three In A Row To deliver a line three times, all on the same take. This procedure is often used for tags. See "Wild."

Throw It Away A direction that means you should be very casual and off-hand with your read; no pushing or "hard sell." I call this approach "buy it or don't, I don't care." (Of course I *do* care, because the client does; but I mustn't sound as though I care *too much*.)

Tone The sound quality of your voice: friendly, harsh, sexy, etc.

Trades An abbreviation for "tradepapers." These publications are a repository of information about the performance industry. They're easily accessible in the three major markets; ask your local magazine store owner for your area's equivalents.

Trendy See "Cutting Edge."

Trio A three-person spot. (Anything requiring more than two actors is often called a "multiple.")

Type An abbreviation of stereotype; a conventional, familiar image of a particular segment of humanity.

Under 1. Music or sound effects "under" means they are heard as an unobtrusive bed for the vocal track. **2.** If you are "under," your read is too short.

Under-Modulate To speak too quietly.

Voice-Over The voice heard in a media project, usually mixed "over" music and sound effects and/or heard "over" a visual.

Voice Print The vocal equivalent of a fingerprint; your unique vocal signature. Experts can positively identify speakers based on analysis of their phonemes.

Volume How loud a sound is.

Vox In a script, another word for voice. (This means you.)

Walla A term for a bed of sound that is composed of many people speaking at once, such as in a restaurant or at a party. If hired for a looping job and directed to supply walla for a scene, do *not* make the mistake of saying "walla, walla, walla," thinking you've done sufficiently specific improv work!

Warm Up 1. To prepare for voice-over work; to "warm up" your voice with exercise and lubrication. **2.** If you're directed to "warm up the copy," adjust your read to make the script more friendly and accessible.

Wet A term meaning a sound with added reverb.

Wild Lines performed out of context. If you read a line "wild," the engineer can place it wherever, and in whatever form it's needed. If you're directed to "Give me three in a row," you're reading "wild," because it's out of the context of the script. Looping work is wild when it's not necessary to be in sync with a specific moving mouth.

Wild Spot A commercial that can run any place, any time, except on cable; that's a "cable spot."

Windscreen See "Pop Filter."

Workstation A digital audio production computer. These machines' digital manipulation of sound is becoming so sophisticated, that some engineers feel they may eventually make "the board" obsolete.

Wrap To finish the job, as in, "That's a wrap!" Your work is done, but don't leave the booth until you're invited to, and never leave the studio until you're released.

Industry Professionals Speak Up

The following are interviews with several of the top people in the voice-over business, who kindly agreed to share their professional opinions and expertise. I deeply appreciate their participation, and I believe you'll find their insights invaluable.

Robin Starr

Voice-over agent with Don Buchwald & Associates, Inc., NY

Robyn works exclusively in voice-overs at one of the largest full-service talent agencies in New York.

Demos and marketing materials

"It's an agent's job to find new talent, so I try to listen to demos that are sent; if I'm really busy my assistant screens them for me. If I'm interested, I'll contact you; if I'm not, I won't. Don't call or e-mail me; I don't have the time to deal with direct follow-ups. A postcard is O.K. but not necessary, because if I want you, I'll call. CDs are convenient, but I don't mind cassettes; I know they're less expensive for those who are just starting to investigate this business, and who haven't made much money in it yet. On that note, I don't require elaborate packaging of your marketing materials; clarity and neatness of presentation are more important. Please remember to put your contact number on the cassette or CD as well as on the case; things can get separated in a busy office, and 'orphan' demos will get tossed.

"As for recruiting, I scout talent in shows, take recommendations from casting directors, coaches and other agents, and attend 'audition evenings' at voice-over schools, where I listen to demos and to actors reading copy. I've discovered some wonderful performers that way."

The voice-over business

"Most agencies in New York will work with freelance talent, but we don't; I focus on finding that 'next big voice,' signing it, and helping it get work. We don't sign so many actors that they end up in competition with each other; our goal is a group of happy, working clients. The voice-over world is small, but not closed; one of the many reasons we like new talent is that we put out an agency demo each year, and want to have some fresh voices on it. Our repeat employers get our CD regularly, and appreciate new sounds.

"The casting process is constantly evolving; it's affected by technology and trends. There are more 'celebrity-voice' spots all the time, therefore fewer for the regular talent pool; smart actors keep up with industry fluctuations and stay flexible so as to remain employed. Keep in mind that the business goes in cycles: the preferred sound for a while will be warm and traditional, then things will shift and everything's 'edgy.' Go with the flow.

"Our character-voice clients know that they have to be extremely versatile in order to have a career in New York, and they are. I can send them to an audition for a talkative pickle or a concerned parent, and be confident of their range."

Positives
"I like actors who know what they're doing; it's called technique. I enjoy nurturing new talent, but I expect beginning actors to do their part by studying and making sure they know how to handle themselves in the booth. Your artistry is a given; I wouldn't be interested in you unless I sensed true talent, but I appreciate your awareness that 'it's called show *business*, not show *art*'."

Negatives
"I'm turned off by performers who think it's all about the voice; acting ability is much more important. If the read has no life, it's just great

pipes saying words, and it won't sell a product. Above all, you must be believable.

"It's unfortunate when actors don't know their strengths and limitations. You should be very selective about what you put on your demo; a spot that's 'just O.K.' dilutes the power of the rest of your material and shows a lack of self-awareness. You shouldn't make a demo until you're able to make one that's a totally effective showcase for your talent."

Advice

"Be very careful about unethical teachers; industry professionals are usually the safest choices, because they're involved in the business on a daily basis and aren't relying on your money for their entire income. I think the *best* studying you can do is the time you spend watching TV and listening to the radio. That's your marketplace, and you must know what's selling and how your talents fit in. Keeping up with pop culture makes you aware of the 'hot' vocal style, and of who has this year's 'celebrity prototype' voice; it's valuable information in a competitive business, so do your research and don't just rely on luck. As I always say, 'Luck is preparation meets opportunity'."

Donald Case

Casting director and owner, Donald Case Casting, NY

Don runs a full-service commercial casting agency, and often gets called upon to handle off-beat, challenging, cartoon/character voice-over audition sessions.

Demos and marketing materials

"I rarely have time to listen to demos, but a nicely handwritten, hand-addressed note sent to remind me sometimes gets my attention. A demo must be professionally produced: *top quality*. Logically, you shouldn't make a demo until you're able to be competitive, so *study*, *train*, and *practice* until you are.

"I have occasionally approached actors who I've seen in shows or other sessions and asked them to audition for a voice-over job, but usually I rely on referrals from trusted agents, coaches and casting colleagues. I've also made calls myself on behalf of talented new-comers. Our industry is all about word-of-mouth, referrals, and repeat business."

The voice-over business

"Having run this casting agency for the past 20 years, I can say that it's extremely rewarding to have lasted this long in a very challenging business. As an 'old pro,' I'm starting to have greater input; clients ask for my opinion and expertise, and that makes my work more satis-fying. In this very tight economic environment, clients sometimes have smaller budgets for casting services than my normal rate; I always say, 'Tell me about your project.' If it excites me, the money is less important than the overall job satisfaction.

"The casting business isn't glamorous: it's about clerical work, organizing, and scheduling. (Sort of your basic drudgery, while remaining 'on' for the client!) But since I recognize that my success has *come* from hard work — knowing the talent pool in New York and keeping up with trends — I just look at it as part of the business. Actors should, too."

Positives

"I like actors who 'bring something to the party.' In other words, they don't walk in blank and wait for me to tell them what to do. I don't do 'rehearsal takes' at auditions; I want to see what you have in mind for the character, and that's 'Take one.' For 'Take two,' I'll give you an extreme adjustment to see if you can turn on a dime and be open to broad-brushstroke direction. If you're good enough to get a 'Take three,' I'll give you a subtle adjustment to check your ability to deal with 'tiny tweaks' of your performance. An actor in complete control of his/her instrument is what I'm looking for.

"In voice-over auditions, I like actors who remember that the voice has to paint the total picture; there are no visuals to aid us, so a 'flat read,' without color or life, is insufficient to sell the product.

"It's great when the talent has a knowledge of basic voice-over technique and terminology; people who claim to be professional actors, but don't know what a 'level' or 'slate' is, annoy me. Actors who present themselves in a professional way — prompt, well-groomed, prepared — show that they respect themselves, me, and the business."

Negatives

"I'm turned off by actors who don't listen; how can they take direction if they don't hear it?

"Don't mark audition scripts in pen; it's inconvenient for the casting director and rude to your fellow actors.

"Don't make noisy page-turns at the mic; unstaple multiple-page scripts so they're manageable.

"Don't think a 'funny voice' is enough; your characters have to be believable.

"Don't beg or whine; develop a grown-up confident manner.

"My pet peeve is actors who have no range, but think they do; they 'offer' me a second read, *exactly* like the one they just did, or don't take an adjustment but think they have. They need to develop some self-awareness.

"Actors who can't divorce 'their souls from their roles' are very difficult to deal with; don't take anything personally; you're in the acting *business*."

Advice

"Competition is fierce; it takes a lot to interest an agent or casting director. A hard-to-find specialty can get you in the door; you can then exhibit your range. A talented newcomer can sometimes win a job with a unique read; don't buy into 'The voice-over business is full of talented people, I'll never break in.' Stay positive: if you become desperate and bitter, it will show in your performance.

"Develop a (tasteful) trademark — an attractive accessory you always wear, a unique vocal specialty, the fact that you're from Tasmania — *whatever*. It helps me remember you; I see thousands of people per year.

"Know that everyone is not cut out for this business; there's no shame in realizing that, and moving on."

Phil Lee

Owner and executive producer, Full House Productions, NY

Phil wears many hats: Full House Studios, part of Full House Productions, creates spots for ad agencies, so Phil often works as the engineer for those; he produces "ESL" (**E**nglish as a **S**econd **L**anguage) tapes, works with voice-over actors on the creation of their demos, teaches workshops, and when clients ask for casting suggestions, he draws on his library of demos and extensive talent network to help them with that aspect of the business.

Demos and marketing materials

"Many voice-over actors send me demos, but I rarely have time to listen; however, if they're recommended by a trusted colleague, that will certainly get my attention. It's O.K. for an actor to send me a reminder about a demo, preferably soon after I've gotten it; otherwise demos pile up quickly and could be thrown away before I get the reminder. I prefer CDs because they're more convenient and getting cheaper all the time. The spots on your demo need to sound real, even if they're not; i.e., they must sound as professionally-produced as an actual commercial. I throw away an unprofessionally-packaged demo immediately, but I also have a negative response to overdone packaging. I don't care for a photo on a voice-over demo, but a picture postcard along *with* the demo, and then used later as a mailing-list tool, does help face/name recognition. I keep about 75 demos in the studio's library, but only about 15 of those are 'active,' meaning the same trusted, experienced actors get called repeatedly. I also keep agency demos, for the convenience of hearing quick samplings of many actors' voices on one CD."

The voice-over business

"Along with the usual commercial production, we seem to do more industrial/narration work all the time, from independent films, to corporate, to books-on-tape, and of course the ESL tapes are a large and specialized part of our business. For that we need very precise dialect work, but having an actor with a good ear, who's flexible and directable, is more important than having a native speaker. There seems to be a larger talent pool of women, so we're always on the lookout for men, particularly young voices, to fulfill the very specific job requirements of this area of the business.

"I'm fortunate in having the opportunity to cast, engineer, and produce many unusual and interesting jobs; I'm also fortunate in the talent pool of imaginative actors who make those jobs fun."

Positives

"The most precious commodity is talent; it's much more important than the sound of the voice. I can manipulate that with technology, but only a true actor can bring a mediocre script to life and 'mine' copy for every iota of value.

"I like performers who don't rest on their laurels, who are always striving to improve their skills.

"Sometimes a commercial is in trouble; in that case, I appreciate it if an actor *politely* offers helpful suggestions for the improvement of the spot. Often a confident, experienced performer can sense what's needed when producers, writers and directors can't.

"Patience is a great virtue in this business, where time, tempers and attention spans are often short.

"I feel that excellence will always find employment; an actor with talent, technique and professionalism will consistently be in demand."

Negatives

"Don't be late, and if you're unavoidably delayed, *always call*. If everyone scheduled for an afternoon audition session is running behind and decides to just not show up, we've wasted a half day of studio time.

"*No attitude*. We're often working on complicated, stressful projects, and we need team players."

Advice

"Be flexible; things change very quickly, so don't get fixated on one idea. Becoming too invested in 'being right,' at the expense of your relationship with the client, can harm your career.

"Don't get defensive; loss of confidence is the kiss of death for an actor. It makes the client, who's probably already nervous, more so.

"If you get a direction you don't understand, try saying 'Could you give me an example?' It indicates an open mind, and invites the client to clarify what's being requested.

"Do your best, control what you can, and then let it go. Nobody's perfect for every job."

Don McGee

Owner and producer, McGee Productions, Inc., NJ

Don is an independent producer, and also a very successful voice-over actor, so he knows the performance business "from both sides of the glass."

Demos and marketing materials

"I try to listen to demos; I can usually tell in the first few seconds whether the performer is viable, so many demos get tossed quickly. My production company is full-service, but focuses on the corporate/industrial world; therefore most of the demos I listen to are geared toward that area. Even in that part of the business though, I appreciate versatility and humor in a demo. Many jobs require character work, and vocal variety can bring life to dry copy. I rarely cast directly from a demo, but a good one might get you an audition. I prefer CDs for their convenience; flashy graphics aren't necessary (and can even look as though you're using 'bells and whistles' to camouflage a lack of talent).

"Please don't call me; it ties up my business line. A postcard to stay in touch is O.K."

The voice-over business

"The state of the economy, coupled with technological advances, have led to consolidation; there are fewer decision-makers involved in any project. The fact that I can be a Producer/Writer/Director/Editor, makes me cost-effective to budget-conscious clients. Anything talent can do to further the 'cost-effective' theme — creativity, versatility, technique — will be greatly appreciated, and keep them in my 'active' file. Familiarity with diverse acting styles, pop-culture references, and specialties, such as dialects and ages, is also very appealing."

Positives

"I like actors who are totally professional: prompt, skilled, dependable, directable, businesslike and pleasant.

"Performers who know their range — who show me their strengths first and then stretch — are very castable.

"When actors return my calls immediately, it tells me that they're interested and conscientious; I respond by giving them as much choice in their audition or booking time as I possibly can. (Narration jobs often go on for days; if you're the first actor to return my call, you can virtually pick your own time.)

"I respond to actors without 'control issues,' who don't resist direction or second-guess the validity of an adjustment. We don't always know *why* an employer wants a seemingly bizarre approach, it's only important that we fulfill the job requirement and end up with a satisfied client.

"It's great when actors (*after* doing what was required), ask, 'May I try something?' It shows interest in the project, and is another chance to demonstrate your script-analysis skills."

Negatives

"Although self-promotion is important, actors who focus completely on their marketing, and ignore their skills enhancement, are missing the point; what you're selling is a lot more important than how you sell it. I call the actor with the greatest ability, not the one who has the fanciest letterhead.

"Actors with an 'attitude of entitlement' don't appeal to me. The world doesn't owe you a voice-over career; you must earn it with talent and hard work.

"A performer who comes in with a 'used-up, burnt-out' demeanor brings negative energy into the session; the talent who is too full of manic energy to listen, is undirectable. Try to find a calm, confident center from which to begin your work."

Advice

"Don't run out of an audition session as though you're embarrassed about your performance; linger briefly in the waiting area while you pack up, check your schedule, etc. The folks in the studio may be discussing your read and deciding whether they need to hear more.

"Remember the importance of people skills. When a terrific actor, with a terrific voice and a terrific personality leaves the studio, we say 'What a nice person.' Of course the talent is important, but what we remember is the humanity. When I give or accept referrals, it's not just the actor, it's the total package."

Pamela's Players

These are the talented voice-over artists heard on the "Talking Funny for Money" CDs. My heartfelt thanks to all for their important contribution to this project.

BRAD BOND
VM (212) 876–9861

Brad Bond enjoys a varied artistic life that includes many aspects of performance, such as acting, directing, and choreographing for the stage. He has also done extensive film work, but particularly enjoys voice-overs. Some of his favorite projects have included looping a 70-year-old Chinese man, Master Fu, in the Fox TV show *WMAC Masters*, and voicing various cartoon characters in *It's Samuel and Nina*, for The Children's Television Workshop. Brad's special skills include proficiency in many dialects, enhanced by his background in languages, such as fluent Spanish, and conversational French and Japanese.

GAI CRAWFORD
VM (212) 229–8360

For years, **Gai Crawford** has been working in the voice-over field in New York and the tri-state area. She focuses on the commercial, corporate and medical narration branches of the business, which make good use of her voice type and articulation. Gai received her MFA in Acting from the University of Michigan, and finds the acting process, techniques and mindset invaluable in the voice-over world. As well as doing her voice work, she teaches public speaking at a NJ state university, and directs musicals for a NJ high school. Gai and her husband live in New York City.

NORMA CREIGHTNEY
VM (917) 593–6695

Norma Creightney, a vice-president at JP Morgan Chase Bank in New York, says: "Pamela's *Talking Funny for Money* workshop raised my confidence level, and enhanced my creativity and imagination in speeches, sales presentations and client interviews. Aside from all that, the fun I had doing character voices was a great stress reliever!" In her free time, Norma volunteers at the Town Hall Civic Association, teaching computer skills to senior citizens. She continues to put her ever-growing stable of character voices to good use reading fairy tales to her beloved niece and nephew.

ROB GORDON
VM (212) 414-5293

Rob Gordon lives in New York City but is originally from the Boston area. His voice-over credits include Luminence Film's *Gettysburg, the Boys in Blue and Gray*, radio commercials such as "The New Jersey Smart Start Buildings Program," and an adaptation of *The Last Unicorn*. Rob is also a comedian, and part of a comic duo called "The Rob and Mark Show." They perform their comedic melodies and general wackiness in New York City, as well as in the tri-state area. "The Rob and Mark Show" recently won the Connecticut Comedy Festival's Third Annual Laugh-Off.

REBECCA HONIG

VM (917) 815–7240

Rebecca Honig moved to New York after receiving her BFA in Acting from Boston University. Once in the city, she took Pamela's *Talking Funny for Money* workshop, and was inspired to begin working in the voice-over field. Since then, she's done voice-over projects for many different producers, such as The Cartoon Network, Bill Plympton, Anime, and ESL. She can also be heard on various network commercials, most recently as the voice of an eight-year-old boy for Laughing Cow Cheese, and is working on a pilot for a new comedy improv radio show at Radio Vision.

PAUL JONES
VM (917) 359-7892

One day, long ago, **Paul Jones** was minding his own business as divisional finance officer for an art auction house, when a producer-friend said, "I'm in a jam. My regular announcer had a sudden schedule conflict and can't make today's booking. You can do this; it's an investment tape for doctors trapped in their BMWs between home, office and hospital." Since that fateful day (and with great coaching from Pamela!), he has been the voice for such clients as Sonoco, Nabisco, McDonalds, ESPN and Bristol Myers. He also does volunteer recording for the blind, and enjoys flying light planes.

KEVIN KOLACK
VM (212) 604–4659

Kevin Kolack has earned a Ph.D. in Chemistry (a truly challenging performance art), and attained certification as a master firefighter. Now a full-time actor, he has been in two dozen independent films and has appeared in stand-up comedy clubs around New York City, in addition to touring the country putting on a one-man, multiple-puppet show. You may hear one of his many voices — from standard announcer, to cartoon mouse, to familiar celebrity — in a variety of television and radio commercials. Recent projects include the award-winning festival darlings *Mutant Aliens* and *H.R. Pukenshette*.

CHRIS LUCAS

VM (212) 874–5300, EXT. 1434

In addition to performing voice-overs for numerous companies, such as AT&T, HBO, Toys "R" Us, MTV, Pfizer, and others, **Chris Lucas** is a very busy stand-up comic and on-camera performer. His stable of over 300 celebrity impersonations and dialects puts him in great demand with casting directors on both coasts. He is also a licensed NYC tour guide and the creator of the award-winning "NJ Sopranos Tour." He is happily married to his wife Candyce, an occupational therapist, who is now used to all the "strange voices" coming from her husband's workshop.

ELLEN MARGULIES

VM (212) 462–9090

Ellen Margulies is the voice of the little green dinosaur in the "Dannon Danimal" yogurt commercials, and the voice of the audio tour of the Jewish Museum in NYC. She's done corporate CDs, political spots and CD-ROM games, and recorded a cartoon series for HBO based on the children's books, *I Spy*. Ellen can be heard as the singing voices of Marilyn Monroe and Marlene Dietrich for "One of a Kind" in Las Vegas. She's been in five Off-Broadway productions, including the long-running *Forbidden Broadway*, spoofing such luminaries as Ethel Merman, Julie Andrews, and Barbra Streisand.

NICK SULLIVAN
VM (917) 312–4609

Nick Sullivan has lent his voice to *Reading Rainbow*, BET's *The Fabulous Reggae Dogs*, and several cartoons for The Children's Television Workshop, in addition to voicing numerous Japanimation movies. He has recorded over 80 audiobooks, receiving two Earphones Awards. Broadway credits include *Footloose*, *White Liars/Black Comedy*, and *The Moliere Comedies*. Nick has worked at numerous American theatres, among them: The Shakespeare Theatre of DC, Goodspeed Opera House, and the New York Shakespeare Festival. On television Nick portrayed *All My Children'* s "Axel Green," and has appeared on *Spin City*, *One Life to Live*, *Law & Order SVU*, and in commercials.

Highlights of the CDs – Revisited

HOW TO BUILD A STRONG, FLEXIBLE, DEPENDABLE VOICE
CD 1, Track 3

To approach this end of the voice-over business, what tools do you need? First, you'll need a strong, flexible, dependable instrument, meaning your voice.

Strong, or it will never make it through an eight-hour film looping day, complete with improvisation, lip-syncing, and blood-curdling screams.

Flexible, or it will never stand up to the demands of cartoon work, where you're expected to talk for numerous characters in the course of an hour-long recording session, shifting constantly. In other words, can you be yourself, your grandma, and your dog, instantly?

Dependable, meaning your voice is ready to go with minimal warm-up, not prone to hoarseness or mouth noise or, heaven forbid, susceptible to chronic laryngitis. But even more important, speaking of dependability, can you be depended on to make bold, brave acting choices, risking peer judgment or embarrassment for the sake of making your work special, and totally committing to your creativity? If the answer is yes, then you're probably wondering how to *get* a strong, flexible, dependable voice.

STRONG

◎ **CD 1, Track 4**

Vocal chords are physiological parts of our bodies, so treat them like any other area in your body that you're trying to build up — with respect but not with fear. "I don't want to hurt my voice" is just an excuse to not do the work. If you warm up methodically, do your exercises every day, and keep your vocal chords well lubricated, they'll strengthen over time.

The Vocal Warm-Up: The grunt-work aspect of the supposedly glamorous world of voice-overs starts here and shouldn't be underestimated. For those of you in the performance business, add these warm-ups to your existing ones. For those just beginning, start with these. You should probably also start looking for a good basic-skills acting class, which will give you more training exercises and will help you acquire the rudimentary technique and terminology you need to be competitive in this highly specialized field.

Staying Lubricated: Professional voice-over actors usually have water with them in the recording studio booth. It helps protect your throat and also helps prevent mouth noise, which can destroy a take. Mouth noise — sibilant "S's," popped "P's," and "B's," clicking sounds, and so on — usually comes from dry mouth, caused by nerves. If it's severe, you can buy imitation saliva at the drug store. If you feel the need for cough drops, avoid menthol and eucalyptus, both of which can have a drying effect. Instead, go for the honey lemon or slippery elm type. Slippery elm tea, found at many health food stores, is also very soothing.

Staying Healthy: Being stuffed up or hoarse means you don't work. So every morning, I use a histamine barrier spray to keep allergies manageable. You can ask your pharmacist about over-the-counter histamine barrier sprays that help keep various allergens at bay. And silly as it may seem, I wash my germy little hands the minute I come in from the world. It helps. If I feel a cold coming on, despite my best efforts, I use a nasal spray with zinc to keep it from getting serious. Again, ask your pharmacist. Remember to follow the standard good health advice: lots of sleep, liquids, a healthy diet, exercise, and moderation with stimulants. All these tips are doubly pertinent in the voice-over world, where a weakened instrument means loss of revenue. So focus, and stay strong.

Strengthening Exercise #1: The Happy Pirates

CD 1, Track 4 features a vocal demonstration of these Strengthening Exercises

You are the entire Happy Pirate family: Papa, Mama, and Baby. They are on the deck of their ship and must project their voices over the noise of sea and wind. They love the pirate life and laugh grandly at every given opportunity. So stand up and inhale a good "tankfull" of air (that means a lung-full).

Papa Pirate says, *Ha, Ha, Ha.*

You try saying it.

Mama Pirate says, *Ha, Ha, Ha.*

Now you.

And Baby Pirate says, *Ha, Ha, Ha.*

Your turn.

And again, using all the voices.

Ha, Ha, Ha.

Ha, Ha, Ha.
Ha, Ha, Ha.

Now practice this exercise awhile, one pirate at a time.

After you've done that, let's put the family together, up and down the scale. It goes:

Ha, Ha, Ha.
Ha, Ha, Ha.
Ha, Ha, Ha.
Ha, Ha, Ha.
Ha, Ha, Ha.

Continue to practice this exercise.

Strengthening Exercise #2: The Russian Bears

CD 1, Track 4 features a vocal demonstration
of these Strengthening Exercises

These bears are huge, aggressive and over-powering, with one line: **Greetings from Soviet Union.** If you already have a Russian dialect, great, but your main effort here is going toward the power, depth, and growl.

Greetings from Soviet Union.

Now you try saying it.

The purpose of this exercise is to enhance the lower part of your chords, to give you a solid base on which to build your range and, hopefully, to give you a couple of lower notes, *since lower notes are money-makers*. Think of all the so-called Voice-of-God announcers and husky-voiced cosmetics spokeswomen. (Or in our end of the business, Darth Vader or Snow White's stepmother!) So try saying, *Greetings from Soviet Union*, lower and lower, until it's not even words — just sound, just growl.

Don't push the volume. Let the mic do its work for you, even if your mic at this point is imaginary. I suggest you do this exercise until you're tired, preferably last thing at night. Then gargle at length with hot salt water, as hot as you can comfortably tolerate with a mild solution of salt, and go to sleep. In the morning you should sound nice and low, with no serious discomfort, because hot salt water is a natural antiseptic/anesthetic and helps heal any minor lesions created by strenuous vocal work.

FLEXIBLE
CD 1, Track 5
Flexibility is important so that you can shift quickly from one sound to another and be cost-effective. You'll hear that phrase a lot — "cost-effective" to a client who's hired you for one hour and expects you to play everyone in his/her project.

Take a look at the Breath Control and Flexibility Exercise on page 21, and listen to the demonstration on **CD 1, Track 5**

As you can see, your three main voices — low, medium and high — are used. To add spice to the mix, I'd like you to do the entire script on one breath. This makes it an exercise to increase breath control as well as to increase flexibility. So try it: take a tankfull of air and read the script all on one breath.

How did you do? If it was difficult, try speeding up. This forces you to shift from voice to voice more quickly and increases flexibility. If it was easy and you had plenty of air left, then slow down and really *act* it. Force yourself to struggle for air at the end, finding that reserve, as we so often have to do in overwritten spots with no commas. Steady aerobic exercise — such as walking, dancing, swimming, or biking — is excellent for breath control and stamina. Flexibility can also be increased by something as simple as reading the entire Sunday comics in as many different voices as you can, as quickly as possible. Don't forget to keep a list of all the voices you come up with during these exercises. One may be perfect at a future audition.

DEPENDABLE

CD 1, Track 6

Can you be counted on to deliver the goods? A huge part of this is your willingness to try; the willingness to look like a fool, as we so charmingly put it. If you're inhibited, insecure, or shy, it's going to be very difficult for you to make the broad, brave performance choices that make you attractive and valuable to a client. Employers often don't know how to get cartoon level out of you, so you have to be willing to look silly and offer it. They can always ask you to tone it down, but you have to offer the broad character first, or they won't know you've got it in you. If you find yourself always going for the subtle, underplayed, naturalistic choice, then the cartoon/character/looping area of voice-overs may be a struggle against your basic instincts. Whereas if you love being larger-than-life and truly enjoy the idea of being goofy for a living, you could become a dependable character-voice actor, someone always willing to go out and swing on the emotional limb — full of ideas, creative, and fearless. If this sounds like you, then you'll need a concrete example of your talent, and that's your second piece of necessary equipment, your demo.

THE DEMO

CD 1, Track 7

A demo tape, or in this day and age, a demo CD, is your primary marketing tool. It's not a place to cut corners. Don't make the mistake of thinking you can save money by assembling your demo in your friend's garage with a hand-held mic. Remember, you're in a competitive, image-driven environment, and you always want to present yourself as you wish to be viewed, a full-time, professional, successful voice-over actor. It's the classic catch-22. You have to spend money before you've made any so you'll look like you don't need any so they'll give you some! The referral sources for training contained on the CD are also useful in choosing a studio in which to record your demo. Prices and quality vary wildly, so be careful, and *picky*.

In my experience, there are three main types of character-voice demos, and all are usually one-and-a-half to three minutes long.

1) **The Story Demo:** In a story demo, you pick a story, one that shows off your best characters, and voice all the characters in that story. Oh, I can hear you now. "I'm not a writer. I'm not clever. I can't think of funny things for my characters to say." *Don't panic.* Maybe you have a friend who can, and will barter. You know — you clean friend's apartment, friend writes you a script — that kind of thing. Just brainstorming with someone is a great way to think up amusing lines, as two minds are better than one. And watching lots of stand-up comedy and comedy skits in general can give you ideas. But if you're at a complete loss, contact me via my website — www.talkingfunnyformoney.com — and I'll try to recommend some talented writers who do this for a living, and enjoy it. But they're not cheap! So give it a shot yourself before you throw money at the problem.

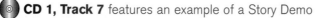 **CD 1, Track 7** features an example of a Story Demo

2) **The Sound Byte Demo:** In a sound byte demo, a character says something amusing, the next character says something amusing, and so on. These characters may be loosely related, but no actual story is being told. A sound byte is short, sweet and to the point. You establish your character and move on to the next one. You want to

show off as many distinct characters as you have as quickly as possible. This exhibits your range and again, cost-effectiveness, which is so important in today's tightly-budgeted market.

CD 1, Track 7 features an example of a Sound Byte Demo

3) **The Combo Demo:** A combo demo is composed of snippets of work you've actually done. (This style might come a little later in your career, of course!) However, don't automatically assume that a real spot you've done is preferable to one that has been created specifically for your demo. While it's lovely to be able to say to a listener, "I was hired to do everything on my demo, they're all real spots," it's actually much more important to have material that shows you off to your best advantage.

CD 1, Track 7 features an example of a Combo Demo

You'll notice I have a thank-you at the end of the demo that serves as a goodbye line. Some actors have these and some don't. Some have introductions. I think there's a natural inclination to begin or end your character demo with your normal voice, just to reassure listeners that you have one. It reminds the listener that you can sound "straight" if necessary (and after all, a straight announcer is just another character). You'll notice I included spots where I perform with male actors; a little dialogue with the opposite sex on your demo can be a good idea. It wakes up the audience's ear and shows you have comic timing and an ability to interact and blend with others.

GETTING TO THE DEMO
CD 1, Track 8

So vocally, how do you acquire the ages, attitudes, dialects, comic timing, emotional availability, and all the other elements that are necessary for assembling a competitive demo like the ones you just heard? Most people aren't born knowing this stuff, so logically you'll need some training.

Basic Acting Technique and Terminology: This can be acquired through professional experience — such as doing plays, readings, films, soaps, commercials — or acquired in the classroom. While you may be gifted with talent, you need to learn to structure that gift so your skills are professional and competitive. Speech therapy can help those with stubborn regionalisms and chronic mouth noise problems. You have to be very committed for this type of self-improvement program to work. It requires many hours of practice outside of class so that the new ways of forming sound go into your muscle memory and become second nature. I've also touched on the necessity of comic timing. This is a tricky thing to learn if it doesn't come naturally, but the first step is immersing yourself in good examples. Listen to recordings of classic radio comedians, such as Jack Benny or Burns and Allen; these are available at many record stores. Try memorizing a section of a classic radio script and doing it with a friend in the exact same rhythm as the original, and see if you can feel the comic timing. Watch classic sitcoms that show up on cable, such as *I Love Lucy* or *The Dick Van Dyke Show*, and you should be able to hear the mastery these actors had over comedy material. You'll notice things are briskly paced but not rushed, energized but not forced. A blend of relaxation and confidence is the key to getting a laugh, just as it's the key to any type of performance. And as I've mentioned before, your relaxation and confidence can be greatly improved by your skills-enhancement training.

Mimicry: A large portion of our cartoon/character/looping work involves mimicking existing sounds. Whether you're asked to sound like a celebrity or an animal or a vacuum cleaner, it's very important that you have what's called a "good ear," meaning you need to be able to hear what something sounds like and replicate it reasonably closely with your voice. This starts with the ability to begin at approximately the same pitch as the sound you're mimicking; you see, all sounds begin on some musical note.

CD 1, Track 8 features a vocal example of mimicry.

As you can tell, there's no end to the easily accessible raw material on which we can practice our mimicry skills. Now many of you might not have had the opportunity to do a lot of singing, so the idea of hearing and replicating a specific pitch may be foreign to you. If so, I suggest trying some singing lessons to demystify the process of hearing and reproducing sound, which is so basic to the work we do. This is obviously not going to be the field of choice for someone without at least the beginnings of a good ear.

Improvisation: Another skill that enhances our voice-over work is what's called improvisational ("improv") ability — the ability to ad lib. Often you'll go into an audition where the client says, "Here's a picture of the character. We haven't written the script yet, so just talk about anything you like, in a voice appropriate for the character, of course. Oh, and be funny." Now, if you're not used to working without a script, this can be intimidating. Fortunately, improv ability can improve with practice, so you might want to consider an improvisation class. The relaxation and confidence you gain from being able to think on your feet may help you come up with the clever line that gets you the job.

Basic Voice-Over Training: This encompasses a few studio techniques, such as:

1) How to speak into a mic to get the most out of your voice.
2) How to analyze copy — that means a script — to tell the story or sell the product.
3) Knowing the basic terminology and etiquette of a recording studio,

so you don't look like an amateur who's never worked in one. (Even if you *are* an amateur who's never worked in one!)

There are many voice-over schools, of widely varying cost and quality, that can help you with the basics. Again, the referral sources of trade papers, service professionals and word-of-mouth can aid you in finding the right fit, and if you contact me via my web site, I'll try to give you an appropriate recommendation. I happen to think a good once-a-week brush-up copy reading class is priceless. A copy reading class means you and several others practice reading various kinds of copy at the microphone with the direction of an instructor. You're handed copy as you would be in a real audition and you have to figure it out. This can be great practice; you get to see what others choose to do with it, so you become aware of whether your choices are competitive, and your instructor can help you with any chronic breathing, articulation, or pronunciation problems.

But most important, it's mic time — invaluable mic time. See, you need time to make the mic your friend. You need to make performing vocally second nature in order to get to a level of relaxation and confidence that means you're competitive. It takes practice, but once you've got it, you're ready to move on to the exercises that are specific to the cartoon/character/looping world.

LOOPING
🔘 **CD 1, Track 9**
Looping is a fascinating but somewhat hidden end of the voice-over business, with very specific technique and terminology. Looping takes place after a movie, commercial, or TV show is filmed. That means it's a part of post-production, and it's related to dubbing. However, whereas dubbing is foreign-to-English — that is, you are replacing the foreign words in a speaker's mouth with English — looping is English-to-English.

There are many reasons for looping. The words in the film actor's mouth are too shrill or the wrong dialect. A plane flew over during filming and obscured dialogue. The director decided after the movie was finished that he just hated an actor's voice — whatever the reason, you, the looper, end up in a studio in front of a mic, watching a screen and lip-syncing new words into the film actor's mouth, line by line. Sometimes you lip-sync a few sounds, sometimes an entire role. Sometimes you're wearing headphones (occasionally referred to as "cans"), depending on the engineer's requirements. Sometimes there's a script for you and sometimes you're expected to lip-read the actor and figure it out.

To practice lip-reading, I suggest that you rent a very talky movie, such as *When Harry Met Sally*, and pick a brief scene between two people with lots of short exchanges. Tape it on your VCR. Pick one of the characters, gender appropriate for you, and practice saying the lines along with the character. When you're comfortable, turn the sound off and try to fit your voice into the character's mouth. (Don't forget to *act* it.) To check yourself, use a tape recorder to record yourself. Play it back as the character's mouth moves — still with the sound off — and see how you did. When it's a perfect fit and your most critical friends feel that your voice is believable coming out of that screen actor's mouth, then you, my friend, have looped. Looped in your own living room, but looped nonetheless!

As well as voicing individual actors, looping also includes providing the sounds of the crowds in movies and providing other background noise. The extras may be miced for what's called a "bed of sound" — the ambiance of the scene — but it's vocal specialists like us who give the crowd the specific vocal energy, words, and therefore vocal feeling that the director has in mind. This vocal feeling may be provided for a broad range of characters and situations — screaming fans at a rock concert, a group of Nobel Prize winners at an upscale party, etc.

Whether it's lip-syncing a specific character or being part of crowd noise, if the scene is playing on the screen while you voice it, it's called "working to picture." You'll also do "wild" lines, which are pre-recorded lines that can be put anywhere in the film whenever they're needed. They are *not* to picture. The most common wild situation involves the "loop group." Loop group refers to all the voice actors who have been hired to loop the particular project. One looper walks up to the mic and firmly plants his/her body — no sounds of shifting feet, rustling clothing, jingling change, or clanking jewelry allowed. The looper says an improvised line, finishes cleanly, and walks away. When the mic is clear, the next looper does the same, goes to the back of the line, and so on.

Sounds easy, doesn't it? Except when it goes on for a long time and it's a small group, so you have little chance to plan what you're going to say before it's your turn again. Trust me — every thought in your head will soon be used up and, of course, the actor in front of you is sure to say the exact line you were planning! So always have a brainfull of back-up lines, because going dry at the mic is the sign of an amateur and won't get you hired back.

Getting Hired for Looping Work: An A.D.R. (**A**utomated **D**ialogue **R**eplacement) editor is hired by the sound editor of a project. The A.D.R. editor needs a certain number of people for looping. That editor either calls voice-over actors directly or enlists the aid of a loop group coordinator. This person calls experienced loopers or might call agents for submissions, take recommendations from trusted colleagues, hire the producer's lover — you know, the usual way things are cast — and assembles the loop group. Small or large, depending on the project, and usually more men than women because a lot of our looping work involves the voicing of police and doctors, still gender-weighted professions. When the loop group coordinator calls you, try to get as much information about the project as possible.

Obviously, if you're going to sound like a lawyer, detective, or archeologist all day, and you haven't had the benefit of that training, you might just want to do a bit of research so as not to dry up at the mic! Of course, all your research time is unpaid, but it can result in impressing employers with your professionalism. And as well, you'll save valuable studio time, which translates to "cost-effectiveness," which can get you hired back.

A looping day is normally from 9 am to 6 pm with an hour off for lunch. It is *intense* because an A.D.R. editor is usually trying to loop an entire movie in one day and stay within the constraints of the post-production budget. Most sessions operate on the "three beep" system, meaning you're watching the screen, it's almost time for you to talk, you hear three beeps, and you speak on the imaginary fourth beep. Your engineer has "laid in" the beeps and you should talk when the beeps indicate, even when you know they are mistimed. The A.D.R. editor should notice, not blame it on you, and retime the beep cues.

You may sometimes be cued with visuals, such as "streamers." A streamer is a band of light traveling across the screen. When it hits a designated point, you talk. Or you may possibly be cued with lights. In this case, you'll see four small lighted bulbs which go out one at a time and you talk on the fourth. The three beep system, however, is most common.

Looping is usually union work because it's for major motion pictures and TV shows. But there are independent films, corporate videos, cable shows, and other productions that require looping and can provide work for the non-union beginner. The loop group does all the voices of all the people in the project who must be looped, so logically you'll need to be incredibly versatile, adept at different ages, dialects, social levels, and so on.

PAADRSC

 CD 1, Tracks 11 – 15; CD 2, Tracks 1 and 2

This is an acronym I've developed to help you remember the different vocal variety options that will enable you to be versatile.

Placement: This means where your sound is placed. I deal with five main areas of placement: Head, Nasal, Adenoidal, Throat, and Chest.

For practice, take a look at the Placement Exercise on page 23 while listening to **CD 1, Track 11.**

Attitude: This is the attitude with which you deliver a line: happy, sad, curious, doubtful, *whatever*. It can change your sound and help give you vocal variety.

Listen to **CD 1, Track 12** for an example of this vocal variety option.

Age: The age that you use for a character, as in baby, teen, adult, senior citizen, etc.

Listen to **CD 1, Track 13** for an example of this vocal variety option.

Dialect: What part of the world is the character from? Those of us in the cartoon/character/looping area of voice-overs are primarily concerned with what I call "Hollywood Dialect," meaning authentic is less important than broad, clear, and funny. If you've had phonetics training, or studied a specific dialect while doing a play, that's excellent groundwork. However, I believe it's far more effective in our business — which is, after all, the pop culture, commercial world — to get your dialects from pop culture. So, for a Hollywood Russian accent, listen to Robin Williams in *Moscow on the Hudson*. For a funny stereotypical German, check out old reruns of *Hogan's Heroes*. Scotty on *Star Trek* does a very accessible Hollywood Scots, meaning you can actually understand what he says. (This is extremely important in selling a product, our ultimate goal!) I'm also very fond of the Hollywood French of Maurice Chevalier, found in movies from the 1950s such as *Gigi*, because although he was actually French, he chose not to use an authentic French accent, which can be too subtle for our purposes or so thick as to be unintelligible. Instead, he opted for clarity and charm, which are much better choices in selling a comic character. If you're doing vocal research, there's probably a movie for every dialect you'll ever need. And of course, I'm a huge Mel Blanc fan. Mel Blanc was the vocal genius behind the Warner Bros. cartoons — Bugs Bunny, Porky Pig, Daffy Duck, etc. — and his dialect work on such characters as Pepe Le Pew and Speedy Gonzalez provides a wonderful vocal model for us: broad, clear, and funny.

For practice, take a look at the Dialect Exercise on page 27 and Hollywood Slavic Exercise on page 29 while listening to **CD 1, Track 14.**

Rhythm: How fast or slow, staccato or steady you say something can give you another vocal variety option.

CD 1, Track 15 features an example of this vocal variety option.

Social Level: What world your character comes from: rich, poor, uneducated, upscale, streetwise, and so on.

CD 2, Track 1 features an example of this vocal variety option.

Celebrities: The ability to sound like a famous person is very attractive in this business and might get you the attention of agents more easily than anything else. Oh, I can hear you now. "I'm not an impressionist. I can't impersonate anyone!" *Don' t panic.* Think: Have you ever been told you sound like someone famous? If so, you're already part way to your first celebrity voice. Everyone sounds *sort* of like somebody else. So tape yourself reading copy in your normal voice, then in your various placements. Have your most critical friends listen and I'll bet someone hears a similarity to a celebrity. For instance, if I'm talking in my chest voice, it's similar to Tallulah Bankhead or Kathleen Turner, and a good place to start working on an impersonation.

The next step is to tape the chosen celebrity. You have to be able to hear a sound over and over in order to mimic it, right? So start your personal library of celebrities whose sounds you're interested in imitating. Keep in mind that while the old favorites (e.g., Katharine Hepburn and Marilyn Monroe for women; Humphrey Bogart and Cary Grant for men) are still popular, you'll constantly get asked for the voices of the stars in the top sitcoms and nighttime dramas, as well as whoever else is prominent in our pop culture. At the time of this writing that would be, for instance, Judge Judy or Regis Philbin — not actors per se, but pop icons nonetheless. And consider musicians, such as Cher and Ozzy Osbourne, for *their* pop icon status. Keeping up with pop culture is a sometimes tedious but absolutely necessary part of our work. Being a snob, as in, "I never watch network television, I don't keep up with modern music, and I certainly never read the funny papers," is an elitist attitude that won't help you in this very commercial business.

CD 2, Track 2 features an example of this vocal variety option.

IS THIS FOR YOU?

CD 2, Tracks 4 and 5

By now you're probably thinking, "No way, this is too much work," or, "It's demanding, but fun. I wonder if I could be competitive." Well, let's recap. You need to:

- Be able to ace all the basic exercises we've worked on so far.
- Be willing to look like a fool in the interest of creating a broad, unique character.
- Be a pop culture maven so that when clients tell you, "Say it like Julia Roberts said it on *Saturday Night Live* last week," you'll know what in the world they're talking about.
- Have a great sense of humor and just plain love acting goofy.

And of course, on top of all that is the ubiquitous grunt-work. Entering the cartoon/character/looping world isn't for the lazy and the effort to remain competitive never ends. There are always new stars to imitate, new talking objects to personalize and bring to life. You can rehearse for *that*, by the way, by talking for inanimate objects around your house. Give each one a voice and a clever line; this is great practice for when they're casting the next talking toilet or chatty cereal.

CD 2, Track 5 features vocal examples.

QUESTIONS TO ASK YOURSELF

How are my people skills?

CD 2, Track 6

I don't mean, "Hey, I'm a nice person." I mean, can you happily shed all your own neuroses and often be the only grownup in the room amidst needy clients, directors, writers, producers, etc.? See, they have the power (and the money). Therefore, it's your job to take all the blame, graciously, for anything that goes wrong. You're allowed no attitude, and must be a master at what we used to call "kissing up." You must be thick-skinned in order to take verbal abuse calmly. It's not that every job experience is negative. Most are great. But you need to be prepared for the occasional toxic situation so you can turn it around to your advantage. And take heart. As I always say, they may treat you like dirt, but if you can hang in there and finish the job, they have to pay you. And the rules of this game are, once you've got their money, you've won!

Do bear in mind, however, that this only works if you're extremely well adjusted. If you know you're overly sensitive to criticism, have a tendency to take things personally, cannot be happily obsequious, then you may want to rethink whether this is an appropriate profession for you. Voice-over actors, character or straight, will always have the lowest status of anyone at the recording session. You must decide if you can live with that.

Do I love to read?
🔘 **CD 2, Track 7**

You will deal constantly with scripts — other people's words — so the English language must be an intimate friend. To be competitive, you have to be able to pick up any copy and read it cold, perfectly. (Your competition can.) No mispronunciation or fumbling over meaning is allowed. Possibly you're thinking, "Oh, I can go early to the audition and practice with the copy." Great plan. You do it. You read beautifully, and the casting director says, "Terrific job. Since you're here, read this" — and hands you a brand new piece of copy, expecting you to read it ice cold. Save yourself embarrassment and be prepared. You can practice cold copy technique by reading aloud into your recorder every day — the more difficult the material the better — and don't forget to *act* it!

Can I be C.I.A.?
🔘 **CD 2, Track 8**

No, not Central Intelligence Agency, but yet another of my acronyms, which stands for "**C**onstantly and **I**nstantly **A**vailable." It's no use having all these skills if the employers can't get you when they need you, right? To be C.I.A. you need two things:

1) A lucrative and flexible survival job. Beginning your cartoon/char-

acter/looping career is just as expensive as starting any new business, what with classes, materials, and so on, and as well as being solvent, you'll also need to be available at a moment's notice for any audition, job, agent meeting, whatever. Nobody needs to deal with your scheduling problems, so unless you're independently wealthy, a lucrative and flexible survival job is imperative.

2) Supportive family and friends. Be assured, you may have not worked for six months, but just as you're sitting down to Grandma's 100th birthday dinner, that's when the phone will ring with a voice-over job. If you're "C.I.A.," you'll take it.

EMPLOYMENT OPPORTUNITIES IN CARTOON/CHARACTER/LOOPING

CD 2, Tracks 9 and 10

Many agents will tell you that if you want to do cartoon work, you must go to L.A. Having done animation work in New York for years, I beg to differ. MTV, Nickelodeon, Public Television, and the Cartoon Network all do some producing in New York. There are also numerous independent animation houses, constantly creating projects they sell to network TV, cable, the educational system, and so on. There will be some cartoon/character work in every market that has voice-overs, from Seattle, Washington, to Washington, DC, but the amount will generally decrease along with the size of the town, which is why so many people interested in this area of voice-overs end up in New York, L.A., or Chicago. Granted, most of the flashy broadcast cartoons — what you see on a Saturday morning — are done in California, and if you insist on having only one or two cute little voices, that's probably where you should go. There are so many funny voices there already for employers to choose from, and so much animation work, that you might just fluke into something by being the new kid in town with your own unique sound. I think a much better choice is to be so versatile you can be cast in cartoons or anything else in the character world.

Cartoons vary in style. Sometimes you'll put words into already-drawn characters' mouths. Sometimes, you'll record a script "wild" — meaning they record your performance and then draw the creature afterward to match your voice. They'll sometimes even film you at the mic and give the cartoon character your mannerisms!

Sometimes you'll dub English into foreign cartoons. For instance, Japanimation, or Anime, is very popular now. The CD-ROM and DVD world has exploded in the last few years, providing many employment opportunities for animation voices. Much of this is for the educational market. And there's also a lot of work in animated educational films — playing teeth that need to be brushed, books that need to be read, etc. A lot of this animated educational work is geared toward the pre-school market and therefore written in a clear, simple style with broad stereotypical characters. They're very good, or very bad, or very silly or very sweet. The subject matter usually contains a lesson about sharing, or honesty, or thoughtfulness. And because it's the educational market, the projects are often very low-budget, which means your versatility and cost-effectiveness can get you the job. It's quite possible you'll be asked to voice every character in the script.

When promos are written in a character style, they need character voices, and that's us. Surprisingly enough, there's also a great deal of character-voice work in the corporate/industrial world. Most of this work is non-broadcast, meaning it will never be on the air. It's mostly made for employees to watch in-house, within the walls of the company, and will probably be shown only once. Think of sales training videos, motivational tapes, insurance plan pitches. Companies churn this stuff out constantly and since it's non-broadcast, a lot of the work is non-union and therefore an excellent place for a beginner to try for a job. Because it's usually very dry material, companies sometimes try to jazz it up with a character approach. For example, a company might do the "which HMO do I choose" scene as a take-off of an old movie, or a pharmaceutical video might be narrated by an adorable little creature named Cecil the Cell.

The wonderful world of modern technology has opened up our job market tremendously. I've voiced phone menus, web sites and automated answering systems, all in the style of the product or company being advertised — therefore making it character work. If I'm voicing an extremely upscale European-based financial institution's phone menu, that's one voice, and if I'm the spokesperson for a web site promoting a new rock band, well, that's quite another!

There's also narration for point-of-purchase videos — those closed circuit TV ads running constantly in stores, usually right by the product display. These ads are very high energy, and again, done in the mood of the product we're talking about. Voice-over actors provide the narration in the headphones (the "audio aids") that guide people through a museum exhibit; we may be the talking dolphin at Sea World or the reincarnation of Martha Washington at Mount Vernon. We provide the voices for Animatics, the animated version of a potential commercial, shown by an ad agency to clients to convince them to come up with the money for the real thing.

Another area of employment is narrating books-on-tape, a fast growing market. A lot of authors use their own voices or celebrities, but character-voice actors often get the fun jobs, the books with lots of extreme character types, ages, dialects, and emotions — the very characteristics you're working on. We also get to do book ads — the commercials made to sell a book — performed in the book's style. So, if the book is larger than life, then logically so is the voice-over style of the actor they hire to talk about it.

Character voices can be called upon for unusual documentary narration jobs, things that would normally go to a straight announcer, but because the subject matter is so bizarre, a need is felt for a uniquely performed read. (Think of some of the documentaries you've seen on the Discovery Channel!) And even when the subject matter *isn't* bizarre, character-voice actors can sometimes snag lucrative announcer jobs just because we've worked on our wonderful chest placement. (Remember that low tones are money-makers?) As I've said, I consider my warm announcer voice to be just another character after all.

Next are bumpers, those corporate sponsor non-ads that you hear at the beginning and end of PBS programs. Bumpers are lucrative and a great showcase for you, since they usually air every week.

Another employment opportunity is ESL tapes, meaning "**E**nglish as a **S**econd **L**anguage" tapes. These are what people listen to when they're trying to learn English. Again, this simple, repetitive material can be very dry, and character-voice actors are often called upon to not only demonstrate what English sounds like when spoken through various dialects, but also to instill the dialogue with humor or drama, and thereby enhance the material.

One of my all time favorite ways to spend my work day is putting voices into talking toys. Have you noticed how many toys talk these days? Wander the aisles of a toy store sometime, push the buttons that activate the electronic chips in the toys, and you'll have an instant awareness of the employment potential. And for every toy that gets manufactured, there are hundreds that don't, that never got past the prototype stage, but a character-voice actor got paid to put words in its mouth anyway!

So, this was a sampling of some of the many employment opportunities for character voices. You're probably thinking, "Great, but how do I market myself so as to get these jobs?" For some suggestions, please check out the following chapter — "Marketing Ideas."

Marketing Ideas

◎ CD 2, Tracks 11 and 12

Many actors make the mistake of sitting by the phone waiting for an agent to call. There's actually quite a bit you can do for yourself, such as reading helpful publications. Several trade papers — *Back Stage, Showbusiness,* etc. — list voice-over jobs, including character work. Occasionally, you'll see P.S.A. (**P**ublic **S**ervice **A**nnouncement) jobs and other non-paid jobs listed, too. Don't automatically reject this performance opportunity, as it could give you mic experience and you might be able to get a copy of the spot for your demo.

I also think it's a great idea to acquire a **B**usiness to **B**usiness, commonly called a "B to B," directory. At the time of this writing, they're free from the phone company, and list lots of establishments that aren't in your regular consumer phone book. See, your mission is to get your demo to a potential employer, and you can start by targeting places that sound like they might have something to do with the entertainment industry, such as film companies, advertising agencies, audio visual companies, and independent producers. One of my best sources of employment is recording studios. Many clients don't want to be bothered with agents, casting sessions — all that money and complexity — they'd rather call a recording studio engineer whom they trust and have him/her cast their spot. So, the client calls with the job requirements, the engineer pulls a few potential demos from his/her files, and auditions only those actors. And wouldn't you like to be in that select group?!

To be chosen, you've first got to get your demo into the engineer's file, right? Again, it's about grunt-work. I suggest using the old sales trick of taking your B to B phone directory and starting at the bottom of the recording studio list, with the "Z's." Most salespeople never get that far, so it's unplowed ground. First, you need to create a company name for yourself; for instance, *Talking Funny for Money* is mine. A company name gives you instant credibility. Doors open much more readily to the name of an organization than to the name of a supplicant actor, so you call the first recording studio and say, "This is Sam Somebody from Sounds Good Productions. I need to talk to whoever there is in charge of your voice-over casting." Now since you sound like a company (and, therefore, a potential employer), rather than a supplicant actor, you have a better chance of actually talking to someone in power. This person might quiz you about your company, so be prepared to chat about it. You're a full-time freelance professional voice-over actor, remember? Therefore, you have the right to give your efforts a professional name. You explain that you just updated your character demo and would like to send this engineer one for his/her files. At this point you may be told, "We don't do any casting here," or, "We're just a music house," or, "We're just a post-production house, tech only." In that case, you thank the person and scratch *that* company off your list. But what if this person says, "Ooh, I'd love to have your demo, but we don't do cartoon/character/looping work here, just straight stuff." Well, try to find out what *kind* of straight stuff, and if you have a commercial, or promo, or corporate demo, then shift gears and start pushing *that*. No sense in wasting the phone call.

But maybe this person says, "Sure, send your character demo. I'll put it in the file." Hooray! You've got your first contact for your character-voice mailing list. Speaking of which, make sure you spell names correctly.

Remember nicknames and personal info from your phone conversation, and get the address right. When you send your demo, enclose your business card, (another very valuable, professional-looking marketing tool), and if you have any work at all to talk about, enclose your voice-over bio. I personally think voice-over résumés are boring to read, whereas with a bio style, the information is more conversational and interesting. You'll see a copy of my voice-over bio below:

VOICE-OVER BIO

Pamela Lewis has talked for just about every kind of creature in commercial/character/cartoon voice-overs, from a chocolate-deprived wimp for Hershey's to the Evil Sorceress for Nintendo video games. She's served as the voices of various crackers for Ritz Bits, spoken for numerous animated characters on the Cartoon Network show *Big Bag,* and done the Chubb Insurance bumpers on *Antiques Roadshow*. She's made a specialty of "baby" voices and has been the baby in national commercials for such products as AT&T, Diet Coke, and American Express. In non-broadcast educational films, industrials, and CD-ROMs/DVDs, Pamela has voiced scores of talking animals, body parts, and inanimate objects, in addition to recording Acoustiguides for museums, and audiocassettes used to teach English in foreign educational systems. She's acted as the voice of numerous electronic toys, been the helpful lady who guides you through your stockbroker's phone menu, and portrayed characters in Talking Books for the Blind. Currently, she serves as the host/narrator for a science series on Public Television and continues to do many political voice-overs (more than 1600 and counting for various national campaigns). As one of New York's busiest "dialogue replacement" specialists, she's acquired extensive experience in dubbing foreign films and looping Hollywood movies, having put hysteria, conversation, and special effects into the mouths of hundreds of screen actors. Pamela has also done looping and promo work for such TV series as *Frasier* and *Homicide*, in addition to HBO, Comedy Central and the Disney Channel. She is based in Manhattan and travels nationwide giving her very popular *Talking Funny for Money* workshops.

I also enclose my picture postcard with my voicemail number. It personalizes my name recognition, and this is their introduction to the face/name/voice "package" that will be contacting them regularly (remember that ever-growing mailing list?) to let them know what I've been doing professionally, that I can't wait to work with them, etc.

Some voice-over organizations sell mailing lists. They may get very specific and say they sell animation marketing lists. Sounds great, like you can skip the B to B directory and cut to the chase. I mean, you'll be calling all the companies in your area that need cartoon/character/looping, right? I wish! Be very careful in spending your money. In my experience, many of these lists have not been "surveyed." In other words, someone has just gone through the phone book and listed all the organizations that sound like they might be viable employers, but no one has actually gone to the trouble of "surveying" them, meaning calling and checking them out. A lot of these lists are rip-offs. I recommend biting the bullet and making peace with the fact that you are your own best P.R. (**P**ublic **R**elations) Director. Speaking of P.R., anything nice that has been said about your talent in print should be packaged professionally and sent to a potential client, along with your demo, business card and voice-over bio.

Remember that I mentioned the character-voice possibilities in the corporate world? These employers can often be approached directly, because they churn out so much material that it's become cost-effective for them to have their own in-house studios and casting directors/producers. Think of all the huge pharmaceutical companies, financial institutions, and insurance firms in your area, and imagine how many sales training presentations, etc. their employees are privileged to "enjoy" every day and you'll get an idea of the voice-over employment potential. And as I mentioned, some of these jobs are for character voices. You need to find out which ones, so I suggest you start your phone calls. Remember, the worst they can do is say no; and they might say yes!

As you're learning about the wonderful world of self-marketing, some great ideas and support can be gotten from a voice-over marketing class. Many of the voice-over schools offer these. Just being able to brainstorm with other cartoon/character/looping voices is stimulating, and can save you time and money, because you can get word-of-mouth recommendations (and rejections) of all these elements of the voice-over world that I've been talking about, such as classes, demo producers, business card printers, etc. And, of course, the best thing about a voice-over marketing class is that it gives you a support system made up of other people in a very specialized field, going through the same things you are.

Now, some folks have decided to take advantage of the computer world to market themselves. They become listed with various voice-over organizations that offer casting services from their websites. Some voice-over actors have websites of their own. If it works for you, great. But remember, I'm not aware of any of this stuff being free, so as the old saying goes, "Before you spend money advertising yourself, make sure you've got something to sell!"

Aside from your own efforts, there are of course agents, managers, and casting directors to aid you in finding work. First you have to get them interested in you, and that again is done through the submission of your demo. There's a publication called *The Ross Reports*, which lists professional agents, managers, and casting directors in the major markets of New York and L.A.; Chicago-based industry professionals are listed in *Act One Reports*. These people can receive literally hundreds of demos a day. Some listen, some don't. Sending a demo cold is a gamble — "cold," meaning they haven't asked for it, and you have no one's name to drop — and *that* means dropping the name of anyone in power who you happen to know, not just those in the entertainment industry. Sending a demo cold is possibly a waste of an expensive tool. Since most agents, unlike the nice folks in your B to B directory, make a point of not wanting you to call them so you can check whether they ever even got — much less listened to — your demo, I think a very good way to ensure that your demo is *at least listened to* is a system that some of the voice-over schools offer. They book in a variety of agents, casting directors, independent producers, etc., each month. You get on the school's mailing list and choose who you want to meet. For a fee, you get a certain amount of time with the guest. You play your demo for this person, sometimes read copy, chat. You're given feedback. You put this industry professional on your mailing list. Whether you're ever called or not, at least you know this person listened to your demo, so even if he/she can't use you right now, you might be recommended to someone else. Good word-of-mouth can be a powerful income-producer.

Speaking of which, *the very best marketing tool* is for you to become, and remain, consistently excellent. That way, anyone you audition for, play your demo for, work for, will become a fan, an unpaid promoter of your talent, happy to refer you to colleagues with more work for you and more referrals, etc., — until one day you realize you actually have a thriving career! Now as you strive to become consistently excellent, don't get so self-absorbed that you forget to listen. If a casting director brings you in for an audition and gives you a direction, but you're fully occupied inside your own head and don't *take* that direction, the casting director will probably assume you're either untalented, stubborn, or stupid. Sad but true; and you don't want any of *those* labels, right? So anything you can do to get to a state of confident relaxation that enables you to hear direction, and produce instant results, is very important to your career marketing. Oh, and never underestimate what I call "the fluke factor." One voice-over actor may do everything exactly by the book — study constantly, have classy materials, market religiously — and get very little payoff, whereas another one lucks into a popular stage show, and the voice-over world is falling all over itself to give that actor a job, whether he/she ever stood in front of a mic before or not. It's a "fluke."

A positive aspect of the fluke factor is that jobs can come out of nowhere, but for that to happen, people have to know about you, and your voice-over life. Therefore, I talk to anyone who will listen — the guy sitting next to me on the train, the dry cleaner, whoever — and I hand out my business card with my voicemail number at every opportunity. I've gotten a lot of work this way. Who knew that the woman I was chatting with in the doctor's waiting room had a cousin who was head of voice-over casting for a major ad agency? She mentioned me to him. He gave me an audition, which turned into a national commercial. Wouldn't have happened if I hadn't talked with, and that's talked *with*, not *at*, that woman, when we were in a non-business environment. But remember, nobody needs a pushy, conceited actor, so keep your voice-over stories amusing and self-deprecating. A combination of charm and humility is very appealing.

Now please return to CD #2, Track #12, for some ideas on "Marketing After You Get the Job."

Lists of Business Contacts in the Three Major Markets

The following lists are a sampling of some industry contacts that I've included for your convenience. Due to the ever-changing nature of the voice-over business, I can't guarantee that these lists are comprehensive, and if I've left anyone out, I apologize.

SAG Franchised Agents

NEW YORK

Agents For The Arts, Inc.
203 West 23rd Street, 3rd Fl.
New York, NY 10011
(212) 229-2562

Amato Theatrical Enterprise, Michael
1650 Broadway, Ste. 307
New York, NY 10019
(212) 247-4456

American International Talent
303 West 42nd Street, Ste. #608
New York, NY 10036
(212) 245-8888

Andreadis Talent Agency, Inc.
119 West 57th Street, Ste. #711
New York, NY 10019
(212) 315-0303

Arcieri & Associates, Inc.
305 Madison Avenue, Ste. 2315
New York, NY 10165
(212) 286-1700

Artist's Agency, Inc.
230 West 55th Street, Ste. 29D
New York, NY 10019
(212) 245-6960

Artists & Audience Entertainment
4 Charles Coleman Boulevard
Pawling, NY 12564
(845) 586-1452

Artists Group East
1650 Broadway, Ste. 610
New York, NY 10019
(212) 586-1452

Associated Booking Corporation
1995 Broadway
New York, NY 10023
(212) 874-2400

Astor Agency, Richard
250 West 57th Street, Ste. 2014
New York, NY 10107
(212) 581-1970

Barry Haft Brown Artists
165 West 46th Street, Ste. 908
New York, NY 10036
(212) 869-9310

Beilin Agency, Peter
230 Park Avenue, Ste. 200
New York, NY 10169
(212) 949-9119

Berman, Boals & Flynn, Inc.
208 West 30th Street, Ste. 401
New York, NY 10001
(212) 868-1068

Bethel Agency
311 West 43rd Street, Ste. 602
New York, NY 10036
(212) 664-0455

Bloc Agency
41 East 11th Street, 11th Fl.
New York, NY 10003
(212) 905-6236

Carlson-Menashe Agency
159 West 25th Street, Ste. 1011
New York, NY 10001
(646) 486-3332

Carry Company
49 West 46th Street, 4th Fl.
New York, NY 10036
(212) 768-2793

Carson Organization, Ltd., The
240 West 44th Street, Penthouse 12
New York, NY 10036
(212) 221-1517

Coleman-Rosenberg
155 East 55th Street, Apt. 5D
New York, NY 10022-4039
(212) 838-0734

Cornerstone Talent Agency
132 West 22nd Street, 4th Fl.
New York, NY 10011
(212) 807-8344

Ginger Dicce Talent Agency, Inc.
56 West 45th Street, Ste. 1100
New York, NY 10036
(212) 869-9650

Eastern Talent Alliance, Inc.
1501 Broadway, Ste. 404
New York, NY 10036
(212) 220-9888

Dulcina Eisen Associates
154 East 61st Street
New York, NY 10021
(212) 355-6617

Flaunt Model Management , Inc.
114 East 32nd Street, Ste. 501
New York, NY 10016
(212) 679-9011

Garber Agency
2 Pennsylvania Plaza, Ste. 1910
New York, NY 10121
(212) 292-4910

Generation TV LLC
20 West 20th Street, Ste. 1008
New York, NY 10011
(646) 230-9491

Barbara Hogenson Agency
165 West End Avenue, Ste. 19C
New York, NY 10023
(212) 874-8084

Archer King
317 West 46th Street, Ste. #3A
New York, NY 10036
(212) 765-3103

Kma Associates
11 Broadway, Rm #1101
New York, NY 10004-1303
(212) 581-4610

Kolstein Talent Agency
85 Lafayette Avenue
Suffern, NY 10901
(845) 357-8301

Lionel Larner, Ltd.
119 West 57th Street, Ste. 1412
New York, NY 10019
(212) 246-3105

Bruce Levy Agency
311 West 43rd Street, Ste. 602
New York, NY 10036
(212) 563-7079

Nicolosi & Company, Inc.
150 West 25th Street, Ste. 1200
New York, NY 10011
(212) 633-1010

Nouvelle Talent Management, Inc.
20 Bethune Street, Ste. 3B
New York, NY 10014
(212) 645-0940

Omnipop, Inc.
55 West Old Country Road
Hicksville, NY 11801
(516) 937-6011

The Meg Pantera Agency
1501 Broadway, Ste. 1508
New York, NY 10036
(212) 278-8366

People New York, Inc.
137 Varick Street, Ste. 402
New York, NY 10012
(212) 941-9800

Premier Talent Associates
1790 Broadway, 10th Fl.
New York, NY 10019
(212) 758-4900

Professional Artists Unltd.
321 West 44th Street, Ste. 605
New York, NY 10036
(212) 247-8770

Pyramid Entertainment Group
89 Fifth Avenue
New York, NY 10003
(212) 242-7274

Radioactive Talent Inc.
240-03 Linden Boulevard
Elmont, NY 11003
(516) 445-9595

Norman Reich Agency
1650 Broadway, Ste. 303
New York, NY 10019
(212) 399-2881

Gilla Roos, Ltd.
16 West 22nd Street, 3rd Fl.
New York, NY 10010
(212) 727-7820

Schuller Talent, Inc.
aka NEW YORK KIDS
276 Fifth Avenue, 10th Fl.
New York, NY 10001
(212) 532-6005

SEM Talent, Inc.
113 Pavonia Avenue
Jersey City, NJ 07310
(212) 330-9146

Tamar Wolbrom, Inc.
130 West 42nd Street, Ste. #707
New York, NY 10036
(212) 398-4595

Michael Thomas Agency, Inc.
134 East 70th Street
New York, NY 10021

Hanns Wolters International Inc.
10 West 37th Street
New York, NY 10018
(212) 714-0100

Ann Wright Representatives, Inc.
165 West 46th Street, Ste. 1105
New York, NY 10036
(212) 764-6770

LOS ANGELES

A S A
4430 Fountain Avenue, Ste. #A
Los Angeles, CA 90029
(323) 662-9787

Above The Line Agency
9200 Sunset Boulevard, Ste. 804
West Hollywood, CA 90069
(310) 859-6115

Activentertainment Talent Agency
325 Smith Robertson Boulevard, Ste. A
Beverly Hills, CA 90211
(310) 289-8200

**Agency West Entertainment,
Talent Agency**
6255 West Sunset Boulevard, Ste. 908
Hollywood, CA 90028
(323) 468-9470

The Agency
1800 Avenue of the Stars, Ste. #1114
Los Angeles, CA 90067
(310) 551-3000

Aimee Entertainment
15840 Ventura Boulevard, Ste. 215
Encino, CA 91436
(818) 783-9115

Allen Talent Agency
3832 Wilshire Boulevard, 2nd Fl.
Los Angeles, CA 90010
(213) 605-1110

**Amatruda Benson & Assoc.,
Talent Agency**
9107 Wilshire Boulevard, Ste. 500
Beverly Hills, CA 90210
(310) 276-1851

Artist Management Agency
1800 East Garry Street, Ste. 101
Santa Ana, CA 92705
(949) 261-7557

Artists Group, Ltd.
10100 Santa Monica Boulevard,
Ste. 2490
Los Angeles, CA 90067
(310) 552-1100

The Austin Agency
6715 Hollywood Boulevard, Ste. 204
Hollywood, CA 90028
(323) 957-4444

Ayres Talent Agency
1826 14th Street, Ste. 101
Santa Monica, CA 90404
(310) 452-0208

Badgley Connor Talent Agency
9229 Sunset Boulevard, Ste. 311
West Hollywood, CA 90069
(310) 278-9313

Baier-Kleinman International
3575 Cahuenga Boulevard West,
Ste. 500
Los Angeles, CA 90068
(323) 874-9800

Baldwin Talent, Inc.
8055 West Manchester Avenue,
Ste. 550
Playa Del Rey, CA 90293
(310) 827-2422

Baron Entertainment, Inc.
5757 Wilshire Boulevard, Ste. 659
Los Angeles, CA 90036
(323) 936-7600

Bicoastal Talent Inc.
8380 Melrose Avenue, Ste. 204
West Hollywood, CA 90069
(323) 512-7755

Bonnie Black Talent Agency
5318 Wilkinson Avenue, #A
Valley Village, CA 91607
(818) 753-5424

The Blake Agency
1327 Ocean Avenue, Ste. J
Santa Monica, CA 90401
(310) 899-9898

Bloc Talent Agency, Inc.
5225 Wilshire Boulevard, Ste. 311
Los Angeles, CA 90036
(323) 954-7730

Brand Model And Talent
1520 Brookhollow, Ste. 39
Santa Ana, CA 92705
(714) 850-1158

**Cassandra Campbell
Models & Talent**
1617 El Centro Avenue, Ste. 19
Los Angeles, CA 90028
(323) 467-1949

Career Artists International
11030 Ventura Boulevard, Ste. #3
Studio City, CA 91604
(818) 980-1315

Castle-Hill Talent Agency
1101 South Orlando Avenue
Los Angeles, CA 90035
(323) 653-3535

Cavaleri & Associates
178 South Victory Boulevard,
Ste. #205
Burbank, CA 91502
(818) 955-9300

**Nancy Chaidez Agency and
Associates Inc.**
6399 Wilshire Boulevard, Ste. 424
Los Angeles, CA 90048
(323) 655-3455

The Charles Agency
11950 Ventura Boulevard, Ste. 3
Studio City, CA 91604
(818) 761-2224

The Chasin Agency
8899 Beverly Boulevard, Ste. #716
Los Angeles, CA 90048
(310) 278-7505

Chateau Billings Talent Agency
5657 Wilshire Boulevard, Ste. 200
Los Angeles, CA 90036
(323) 965-5432

W. Randolph Clark Company
13415 Ventura Boulevard, Ste. 3
Sherman Oaks, CA 91423
(818) 385-0583

Colleen Cler Agency Inc.
178 South Victory, Ste. #108
Burbank, CA 91502
(818) 841-7943

Contemporary Artists, Ltd.
610 Santa Monica Boulevard, Ste. 202
Santa Monica, CA 90401
(310) 395-1800

The Coppage Company
5411 Camellia Avenue
North Hollywood, CA 91601
(818) 980-8806

Coralie Jr. Theatrical Agency
4789 Vineland Avenue, Ste. #100
North Hollywood, CA 91602
(818) 766-9501

The Dangerfield Agency
4053 Radford Avenue, Ste. C
Studio City, CA 91604
(818) 766-7717

Craig S Dorfman & Associates
6100 Wilshire Boulevard, Ste. 310
Los Angeles, CA 90048
(323) 937-8600

Dragon Talent Inc.
8444 Wilshire Boulevard,
Penthouse Ste.
Los Angeles, CA 90211
(323) 653-0366

EBS Los Angeles
3000 West Olympic Boulevard,
Ste. 1435
Santa Monica, CA 90404
(310) 449-4065

**Elite of Los Angeles
Talent Agency**
345 North Maple Drive, Ste. #397
Beverly Hills, CA 90210
(310) 274-9395

Ellechante Talent Agency
274 Spazier Avenue
Burbank, CA 91502
(323) 750-9490

Ellis Talent Group
14241 Ventura Boulevard, Ste. 207
Sherman Oaks CA 91423
(818) 501-7447

Equinox Models and Talent
8961 Sunset Boulevard,
Penthouse Ste.
West Hollywood, CA 90069
(323) 951-7100

Evolve Talent, Talent Agency
445 South Figueroa Street, Ste. 2600
Los Angeles, CA 90071
(323) 467-3376

**Ferrar Media Associates,
Talent Agency**
8430 Santa Monica Boulevard,
Ste. 220
Los Angeles, CA 90069
(323) 654-2601

Film Artists Associates
4717 Van Nuys Boulevard, Ste. 215
Sherman Oaks, CA 91403
(818) 386-9669

Flick East & West Talents, Inc.
9057 Nemo Street, Ste. #A
West Hollywood, CA 90069
(310) 271-9111

**Fontaine Agency/Hero,
Talent Agency**
205 South Beverly Drive, Ste. 212
Beverly Hills, CA 90212
(310) 275-4620

Barry Freed Company
2040 Avenue of the Stars, Ste. 400
Los Angeles, CA 90067
(310) 860-5627

Alice Fries Agency
1927 Vista Del Mar Avenue
Los Angeles, CA 90068
(323) 464-1404

The Geddes Agency
8430 Santa Monica Boulevard, #200
West Hollywood, CA 90069
(323) 848-2700

Laya Gelff Agency
16133 Ventura Boulevard, Ste. #700
Encino, CA 91436
(818) 996-3100

Paul Gerard Talent Agency
11712 Moorpark Street, Ste. 112
Studio City, CA 91604
(818) 769-7015

Don Gerler Agency
3349 Cahuenga Boulevard West,
Ste. #1
Los Angeles, CA 90068
(323) 850-7386

Michelle Gordon & Associates
260 South Beverly Drive, Ste. 308
Beverly Hills, CA 90212
(310) 246-9930

GRA/Gordon Rael Agency,LLC
9242 Beverly Boulevard, 3rd Fl.
Beverly Hills, CA 90210
(310) 786-7427

Grant, Savic, Kopaloff and Associates
6399 Wilshire Boulevard, Ste. 414
Los Angeles, CA 90048
(323) 782-1854

Greene & Associates
526 North Larchmont Boulevard,
Ste. 201
Los Angeles, CA 90004
(323) 960-1333

Halpern & Associates
12304 Santa Monica Boulevard,
Ste. 104
Los Angeles, CA 90025
(310) 571-4488

Mitchell J. Hamilburg Agency
8671 Wilshire Boulevard, Ste. 500
Beverly Hills, CA 90211
(310) 471-4024

Vaughn D. Hart & Associates
8899 Beverly Boulevard, Ste. #815
Los Angeles, CA 90048
(310) 273-7887

Hervey/Grimes Talent Agency
10561 Missouri, #2
Los Angeles, CA 90025
(310) 475-2010

Hilltop Talent Agency
27520 Hawthorne Boulevard, Ste. 133
Rolling Hills Estates, CA 90274
(310) 265-0611

Daniel Hoff Agency
1800 North Highland Avenue,
Ste. #300
Los Angeles, CA 90028
(323) 962-6643

Hollander Talent Group, Inc.
14011 Ventura Boulevard, Ste. 202
Sherman Oaks, CA 91423
(818) 382-9800

Icon Talent Agency
1717 West Magnolia Boulevard,
Ste. 100
Burbank, CA 91505
(818) 526-1444

IFA Talent Agency
8730 Sunset Boulevard, Ste. 490
Los Angeles, CA 90069
(310) 659-5522

George Jay Agency
6269 Selma Avenue, Ste. 15
Los Angeles, CA 90028
(323) 466-6665

The Susan Johnson Talent Agency
13321 Ventura Boulevard, Ste. C-1
Sherman Oaks, CA 91423
(818) 986-2205

JS Represents, Talent Agency
6815 Willoughby Avenue, Ste. 104
Los Angeles, CA 90036
(323) 462-3246

Sharon Kemp Talent Agency
447 South Robertson Boulevard,
Ste. 204
Beverly Hills, CA 90211
(310) 858-7200

Kerwin William Agency
1605 North Cahuenga Boulevard,
Ste. #202
Los Angeles, CA 90028
(323) 469-5155

Eric Klass Agency
139 South Beverly Drive, Ste. 331
Beverly Hills, CA 90212
(310) 274-9169

KM and Associates, Talent Agency
4922 Vineland Avenue,
North Hollywood, CA 91601
(818) 766-3566

Leavitt Talent Group
6404 Wilshire Boulevard, Ste. 950
Los Angeles, CA 90048
(323) 658-8118

The Levin Agency
8484 Wilshire Boulevard, Ste. 750
Beverly Hills, CA 90211
(323) 653-7073

Robin Levy & Associates
9220 Sunset Boulevard, Ste. 305
Los Angeles, CA 90069
(310) 278-8748

Robert Light Agency
6404 Wilshire Boulevard, Ste. 900
Los Angeles, CA 90048
(323) 651-1777

LJ and Associates
7949 Woodley Avenue, Ste. 102
Van Nuys CA 91406
(818) 345-9274

Jana Luker Talent Agency
1923 1/2 Westwood Boulevard,
Ste. #3
Los Angeles, CA 90025
(310) 441-2822

LW 1, Inc.
8383 Wilshire Boulevard, Ste. 649
Beverly Hills, CA 90211
 (323) 653-5700

Lynne & Reilly Agency
Toluca Plaza Building
10725 Vanowen Street, Ste. 113
North Hollywood, CA 91605
(323) 850-1984

Mademoiselle Talent Agency
10835 Santa Monica Boulevard,
Ste. 204-A
Los Angeles, CA 90025
(310) 441-9994

Malaky International
10642 Santa Monica Boulevard,
Ste. 103
Los Angeles, CA 90025
(310) 234-9114

Alese Marshall
Model & Comml Agncy
22730 Hawthorne Boulevard, Ste. 201
Torrance, CA 90505
(310) 378-1223

Maxine's Talent Agency
4830 Encino Avenue
Encino, CA 91316
(818) 986-2946

Media Artists Group
6404 Wilshire Boulevard, Ste. 950
Los Angeles, CA 90048
(323) 658-5050

Meridian Artists Agency
9229 Sunset Boulevard, Ste. 310
Los Angeles, CA 90069
(310) 246-2600

MGA/Mary Grady Agency
221 East Walnut Street, Ste. 130
Pasadena, CA 91101
(818) 567-1400

Miramar Talent Agency
7400 Beverly Boulevard,
Ste. 220
Los Angeles, CA 90036
(323) 934-0700

The Models Guild of California
8489 West 3rd Street, Ste. 1106,
1107 & 1109
Los Angeles, CA 90048
(323) 801-2132

Morgan Agency
7080 Hollywood Boulevard, Ste. 1009
Hollywood, CA 90028
(323) 469-7100

H David Moss & Assoc.
733 North Seward Street, Penthouse
Los Angeles, CA 90038
(323) 465-1234

N T A Talent Agency
8899 Beverly Boulevard, Ste. 612
Los Angeles, CA 90048
(310) 274-6297

Nu Talent Agency
117 North Robertson Boulevard,
Los Angeles, CA 90048
(310) 385-6907

Omnipop Inc.
10700 Ventura Boulevard,
Second Fl., Ste. 2C
Studio City, CA 91604
(818) 980-9267

Origin Talent, Talent Agency
3393 Barham Blvd
Los Angeles, CA 90068
(323) 845-4141

Cindy Osbrink Talent Agency
4343 Lankershim Boulevard, Ste. 100
Universal City, CA 91602
(818) 760-2488

Otis, Dorothy Day Partners
215 S La Cienega Boulevard,
Penthouse Ste. 209
Beverly Hills, CA 90211
(323) 782-0070

Pacific West Artists Talent Agency
12500 Riverside Drive, Ste. 202
Valley Village, CA 91607
(818) 755-8544

Pakula King & Associates
9229 Sunset Boulevard, Ste. 315
Los Angeles, CA 90069
(310) 281-4868

Partos Company, The
6363 Wilshire Boulevard, Ste. 227
Los Angeles, CA 90048
(310) 458-7800

Peak Models & Talent
28065 Avenue Stanford
Valencia, CA 91355
(661) 288-1555

Pierce Agency, John
8380 Melrose Avenue, Ste. 106
West Hollywood, CA 90069
(323) 653-3976

Pinnacle Commercial Talent
5757 Wilshire Boulevard, Ste. 510
Los Angeles, CA 90036
(323) 939-5440

Players Talent Agency
13033 Ventura Boulevard, Ste. N
Studio City, CA 91604
(818) 528-7444

Privilege Talent Agency
14542 Ventura Boulevard, Ste. 209
Sherman Oaks, CA 91403
(818) 386-2377

Progressive Artists
400 S Beverly Drive, Ste. #216
Beverly Hills, CA 90212
(310) 553-8561

Q Model Management
6100 Wilshire Boulevard, Ste. 710
Los Angeles, CA 90048
(323) 692-1700

Qualita Dell'Arte
5353 Topanga Canyon Road, Ste. 220
Woodland Hills, CA 91364
(818) 598-8073

Cindy Romano
Modeling & Talent Agency
414 Village Square West
Palm Springs, CA 92262
(760) 323-3333

S D B Partners, Inc.
1801 Avenue of the Stars, Ste. 902
Los Angeles, CA 90067
(310) 785-0060

Michael Salazar Agency
1436 South La Cienega Boulevard,
Ste. 207
Los Angeles, CA 90035
(310) 659-3030

Samantha Group, Talent Agency
300 South Raymond Avenue, Ste. 11
Pasadena, CA 91105
(626) 683-2444

Sarnoff Company, Inc.
10 Universal City Plaza, Ste. 2000
Universal City, CA 91608
(818) 973-4555

Jack Scagnetti Talent Agency
5118 Vineland Avenue, Ste. 102
North Hollywood, CA 91601
(818) 762-3871

The Irv Schechter Company
9300 Wilshire Boulevard, Ste. 400
Beverly Hills, CA 90212
(310) 278-8070

Sandie Schnarr Talent
8500 Melrose Avenue, Ste. 212
West Hollywood, CA 90069
(310) 360-7680

Schultz/Carroll Associates
6442 Coldwater Canyon, Ste. 206
North Hollywood, CA 91606
(818) 760-3100

Schwartz Associates, Don
1604 North Cahuenga Boulevard,
Ste. 101
Los Angeles, CA 90028
(323) 464-4366

Screen Artists Agency
12435 Oxnard Street
North Hollywood, CA 91606
(818) 789-4896

**Select Model & Talent
Agency(SMT) LLC**
8271 Melrose Avenue, Ste. 203
Los Angeles, CA 90046
(323) 653-6732

Shapira & Assoc.
15821 Ventura Boulevard, Ste. 235
Encino, CA 91436
(818) 906-0322

**Shapiro-Lichtman Inc.,
Talent Agency**
8827 Beverly Boulevard,
Los Angeles, CA 90048
(310) 859-8877

Jerome Siegel Associates
1680 North Vine Street, Ste. 613
Hollywood, CA 90028
(323) 466-0185

Sierra Talent Agency
14542 Ventura Boulevard, Ste. 207
Sherman Oaks, CA 91403
(818) 907-9645

Signature Artists Agency
6700 West 5th Street
Los Angeles, CA 90048
(323) 651-0600

Michael Slessinger Assoc.
8730 Sunset Boulevard, Ste. 220
West Hollywood, CA 90069
(310) 657-7113

The Sohl Agency
669 Berendo Street
Los Angeles, CA 90004
(323) 644-0500

Camille Sorice Talent Agency
13412 Moorpark Street, Ste. C
Sherman Oaks, CA 91423
(818) 995-1775

Scott Stander & Associates Inc.
13701 Riverside Drive, Ste. 201
Sherman Oaks, CA 91423
(818) 905-7000

Starcraft, Talent Agency
3330 Barham, Ste. 105
Los Angeles, CA 90068
(323) 845-4784

Starwill Talent Agency
433 North Camden Drive, 4th Fl.
Beverly Hills, CA 90210
(323) 874-1239

Charles H. Stern Agency
11845 West Olympic Boulevard,
Ste. 1177
Los Angeles, CA 90064
(310) 476-5244

The Stevens Group
14011 Ventura Boulevard, Ste. 201
Sherman Oaks CA 91423
(818) 528-3674

Superior Talent Agency
11425 Moorpark Street
Studio City, CA 91602
(818) 508-5627

Talent Syndicate, LLC
1680 North Vine Street, Ste. 614
Los Angeles, CA 90028
(323) 463-7300

Thomas Talent Agency
6709 La Tijera Boulevard, Ste. 915
Los Angeles, CA 90045
(310) 665-0000

**Arlene Thornton
& Associates, Arlene**
12711 Ventura Boulevard, Ste. 490
Studio City, CA 91604
(818) 760-6688

Tilmar Talent Agency
4929 Wilshire Boulevard, Ste. 830
Los Angeles, CA 90010
(323) 938-9815

Tisherman Agency, Inc.
6767 Forest Lawn Drive, Ste. 101
Los Angeles, CA 90068
(323) 850-6767

United Artists Talent Agency
14011 Ventura Boulevard, Ste. 213
Sherman Oaks, CA 91423
(818) 788-7305

US Talent Agency
485 S Robertson Boulevard, Ste. 7
Beverly Hills, CA 90211
(310) 858-1533

VE Model & Talent Agency
3015 Main Street, Ste. 460
Santa Monica, CA 90405
(310) 399-9800

Vision Art Management
9200 Sunset Boulevard, Penthouse 1
Los Angeles, CA 90069
(310) 888-3288

Wallis Agency
4444 Riverside Drive, Ste. 105
Burbank, CA 91505
(818) 953-4848

Bob Waters Agency Inc.
9301 Wilshire Boulevard, Ste. 300
Beverly Hills, CA 90210
(310) 777-8277

Ann Waugh Talent Agency
4741 Laurel Canyon Boulevard,
Ste. 200
Valley Village, CA 91607
(818) 980-0141

Shirley Wilson & Associates
5410 Wilshire Boulevard, Ste. #806
Los Angeles, CA 90036
(323) 857-6977

Zanuck, Passon & Pace
13317 Ventura Boulevard, Ste. I
Sherman Oaks, CA 91423
(818) 783-4890

CHICAGO

Ambassador Talent Agents
333 North Michigan Avenue, Ste. 910
Chicago, IL 60601
(312) 641-3491

Aria Model & Talent Mgmt.
1017 West Washington Street, #2C
Chicago, IL 60607
(312) 243-9400

Baker & Rowley
Talent Agency, Inc.
1327 West Washington Street,
Ste. 5-C
Chicago, IL 60607-1914
(312) 850-4700

Big Mouth Talent
935 West Chestnut Street, Ste. 415
Chicago, IL 60622
(312) 421-4400

E T A Inc.
7558 South Chicago Avenue
Chicago, IL 60619
(773) 752-3955

Encore Talent Agency, Inc.
1532 North Milwaukee Street,
#204-205
Chicago, IL 60622
(773) 384-7300

Ford Talent Group, Inc.
641 West Lake Street, Ste. 402
Chicago, IL 60661
(312) 707-9000

Geddes Agency
1633 North Halsted Street, Ste. 400
Chicago, IL 60614
(312) 787-8333

Shirley Hamilton
333 East Ontario Street, Ste. B
Chicago, IL 60611
(312) 787-4700

Linda Jack Talent
230 East Ohio Street, Ste. #200
Chicago, IL 60611
(312) 587-1155

Lily's Talent Agency
1301 West Washington Street, Ste. B
Chicago, IL 60607
(312) 601-2345

Naked Voices, Inc.
865 North Sangamon Avenue,
Ste. 415
Chicago, IL 60622
(312) 563-0136

Salazar & Navas, Inc.
760 North Ogden Avenue, Ste. 2200
Chicago, IL 60622
(312) 751-3419

Schucart, Norman Ent
1417 Green Bay Road,
Highland Park IL 60035-3614
(847) 433-1113

Stewart Talent Management
58 West Huron Street,
Chicago, IL 60610
(312) 943-3131

Third Coast Artists, Inc.
641 West Lake Street, Ste. 402
Chicago, IL 60661
(312) 670-4444

Voices Unlimited, Inc.
541 North Fairbanks Court, Ste. 2735
Chicago, IL 60611-3319
(312) 832-1113

Arlene Wilson Talent, Inc.
430 West Erie Street, Ste. #210
Chicago, IL 60610
(312) 573-0200

AFTRA Franchised Agents

NEW YORK

About Artists Agency
1650 Broadway, Ste. 1406
New York, NY 10019
(212) 490-7191

Abrams Artists & Assoc.
275 Seventh Avenue, 26th Fl.
New York, NY 10001
646-486-4600

Access Talent, Inc.
37 East 28th Street, Ste. 500
New York, NY 10016
(212) 684-7795

Acme Talent & Literary
875 Avenue of the Americas,
Ste. 2108
New York, NY 10001
(212) 328-0388

Atlas Talent Agency, Inc.
36 West 44th Street, Ste. 1000
New York, NY 10036
212-730-4500

Bret Adams Ltd.
448 44th Street
New York, NY 10036
(212) 765-5630

Agents for the Arts, Inc.
203 West 23rd Street, 3rd Fl.
New York, NY 10011
(212) 229-2562

Michael Amato Agency
1650 Broadway, Rm. #307
New York, NY 10019
(212) 247-4456

American Int'l Talent Agency
303 West 42nd Street, #608
New York, NY 10036
(212) 245-8888

Beverly Anderson
1501 Broadway, #2008
New York, NY 10036
(212) 944-7773

Andreadis Talent Agency
119 West 57th Street, #711
New York, NY 10019
(212) 315-0303
All Areas

Arcieri & Associates
305 Madison Avenue, Ste. 2315
New York, NY 10165
(212) 286-1700

Artist's Agency Inc.
230 West 55th Street
New York, NY 10019
(212) 245-6960

The Artists Group East
1650 Broadway, Ste. 711
New York, NY 10019
(212) 586-1452

Associated Booking Corp.
1995 Broadway, #501
New York, NY 10023
(212) 874-2400

The Richard Astor Agency
250 West 57th Street, #2014
New York, NY 10107
(212) 581-1970

Barry Haft Brown Artists Agency
165 West 46th Street, #908
New York, NY 10036
(212) 869-9310

Bauman Redanty & Shaul
250 West 57th Street, #473
New York, NY 10019
(212) 757-0098

Peter Beilin Agency Inc.
230 Park Avenue, Rm. #923
New York, NY 10169
(212) 949-9119

The Bethel Agency
311 West 43rd Street, Ste. 602
New York, NY 10036
(212) 664-0455

Berman, Boals & Flynn, Inc.
230 West 30th Street, Ste. 401
New York, NY 10001
(212) 868-1068

N.S. Bienstock Inc.
1740 Broadway, 24th Fl.
New York, NY 10019
(212) 765-3040

Don Buchwald & Assoc.
10 East 44th Street
New York, NY 10017
(212) 867-1200

Carlson-Menashe Artists
149 5th Avenue, #1204
New York, NY 10010
212-228-8826

Carry Company
49 West 46th Street, 4th Fl.
New York, NY 10036
(212) 768-2793

Carson-Adler Agency, Inc.
250 West 57th Street
New York, NY 10107
(212) 307-1882

The Carson Organization Ltd.
240 West 44th Street, PH
New York, NY 10036
(212) 221-1517

Coleman-Rosenberg
155 East 55th Street, 5D
New York, NY 10022
(212) 838-0734

Columbia Artists Management
165 West 57th Street
New York, NY 10019
(212) 397-6900

Cornerstone Talent Agency
132 West 22nd Street, 4th Fl.
New York, NY 10011
(212) 807-8344

**Cunningham, Escott,
Dipene & Assoc.**
257 Park Avenue South, Ste. 900
New York, NY 10010
(212) 477-1666

Ginger Dicce Talent Agency
1650 Broadway, #714
New York, NY 10019
(212) 974-7455

**Douglas, Gorman,
Rothacker & Wilhelm, Inc.**
1501 Broadway, #703
New York, NY 10036
(212) 382-2000

Dulcina Eisen Associates
154 East 61st Street
New York, NY 10021
(212) 355-6617

Eastern Talent Alliance
1501 Broadway, Ste. 404
New York, NY 10036
(212) 840-6868

Endeavor Agency, LLC
270 Lafayette Street, Ste. 605
New York, NY 10012
(212) 625-2500

EWCR & Associates
311 West 43rd Street, #304
New York, NY 10036
(212) 586-9110

Famous Artists Agency Inc.
1700 Broadway
New York, NY 10019
(212) 245-3939

Flaunt Model Management
114 East 32nd Street
New York, NY 10016
(212) 679-9011

Fresh Faces Agency, Inc.
108 South Franklin Avenue, Ste. 11
Valley Stream, NY 11580
(516) 223-0034

Fronteir Booking Int'l, Inc.
1560 Broadway, #1110
New York, NY 10036
(212) 221-0220

The Gage Group
315 West 57th Street, #4H
New York, NY 10019
(212) 541-5250

Garber Talent Agency
2 Penn Plaza
New York, NY 10121-0099
(212) 292-4910

Generation TV
20 West 20th Street, #1008
New York, NY 10011
(646) 230-9491

The Gersh Agency NY Inc.
130 West 42nd Street, #2400
New York, NY 10036
(212) 997-1818

Peggy Hadley Enterprises Ltd.
250 West 57th Street, Ste. 2317
New York, NY 10107
(212) 246-2166

Harden-Curtis Associates
850 Seventh Avenue, #405
New York, NY 10019
(212) 977-8502

Hartig-Hilpeo Agency, Ltd.
156 Fifth Avenue, Ste. 820
New York, NY 10010
(212) 929-1772

Henderson/Hogan Agency, Inc.
850 Seventh Avenue, #1003
New York, NY 10019
(212) 765-5190

The Barbara Hogenson Agency
165 West End Avenue, Ste. 19-C
New York, NY 10023
(212) 874-8084

HWA Talent Representatives
220 East 23rd Street, #400
New York, NY 10010
(212) 889-0800

Ingber & Associates
274 Madison Avenue, Ste. 1104
New York, NY 10016
(212) 889-9450

**Innovative Artists
Talent & Literary Agency**
141 5th Avenue, 3rd Fl. South
New York, NY 10010
(212) 253-6900

**International Creative Mgt.
(I.C.M.)**
40 West 57th Street
New York, NY 10019
(212) 556-5600

**Jordan, Gill & Dornbaum
Agency, Inc.**
1133 Broadway, Ste. 623
New York, NY 10010
(212) 463-8455

Stanley Kaplan Talent
139 Fulton Street, Ste. 503
New York, NY 10038
(212) 385-4400

Kazarian/Spencer & Assoc., Inc.
162 West 56th Street, Ste. 307
New York, NY 10019
(212) 582-7572

Kerin-Goldberg Associates
155 East 55th Street, #5D
New York, NY 10022
(212) 838-7373

Archer King, Ltd.
317 West 46th Street, Ste. 3A
New York, NY 10035
(212) 765-3103

**Kolstein Talent Agency, dba
Naomi's World Entertainment, Inc.**
85 C Lafayette Avenue
Suffern, NY 10901
(845) 357-8301

The Krasny Office, Inc.
1501 Broadway, #1303
New York, NY 10036
(212) 730-8160

L.B.H. Assoc., Inc.
20 West 64th Street, Apt. 302
New York, NY 10023
(212) 501-8936

Lally Talent Agency
630 Ninth Avenue, #800
New York, NY 10036
(212) 974-8718

The Lantz Office
200 West 57th Street, # 503
New York, NY 10019
(212) 586-0200

Lionel Larner, Ltd.
119 West 57th Street, Ste. 1412
New York, NY 10019
(212) 246-3105

Bernard Liebhaber Agency
352 Seventh Avenue, 7th Fl.
New York, NY 10001
212-631-7561

The Leudtke Agency
1674 Broadway, Ste. 7A
New York, NY 10019
(212) 220-3532

Bruce Levy Agency
311 West 43rd Street, #602
New York, NY 10036,
(212) 262-6845

Maresca Talent Agency
1169 Main Street, Ste. A-7
Branford, CT 06405
(203) 481-0547

McCullough Associates
8 South Hanover Avenue
Margate, NJ 08402
(609) 822-2222

Meredith Model Mgmt.
10 Furler Street
Totawa, NJ 07512
(651) 812-0122

JMA – The Jack Menashe Agency
160 East 61st Street, 3rd Fl.
New York, NY 10021
(212) 588-0902/0903

William Morris Agency
1325 Avenue of The Americas
New York, NY 10019
(212) 586-5100

Nicolisi & Company, Inc.
150 West 25th Street, Ste. 1200
New York, NY 10001
(212) 633-1010

Nouvelle Talent Inc.
20 Bethune Street, #4A
New York, NY 10014
(212) 645- 0940

Omnipop Inc., Talent Agency
55 West Old Country Rd.
Hicksville, NY 11801
(516) 937-6011

Fifi Oscard Agency, Inc.
110 West 40th Street
New York, NY 10018
(212) 764-1100

Paradigm
200 West 57th Street, #900
New York, NY 10019
(212) 246-1030

Professional Artists Unlimited
321 West 44th Street, Ste. 605
New York, NY 10036
(212) 247-8770

Pyramid Entertainment
89 Fifth Avenue.
New York, NY 10003
(212) 242-7274

Radioactive Talent Inc.
350 Third Avenue, Ste. 400
New York, NY 10010

Norman Reich Agency, Inc.
1650 Broadway, Ste. 303
New York, NY 10019
(212) 399-2881

Gilla Roos Ltd.
16 West 22nd Street, 3rd Fl.
New York, NY 10010
(212) 727-7820

Sames & Rollnick Assoc.
250 West 57th Street, Ste. 810
New York, NY 10107
(212) 315-4434

The Sanders Agency Ltd.
1204 Broadway, #306
New York, NY 10001
(212) 779-3737

William Schill Agency, Inc.
302A West 12th Street, #183
New York, NY 10014
(877) 813-3923

Schiowitz/Clay/Rose
165 West 46th Street, Ste. 1210
New York, NY 10036
(212) 840-6787

Schuller Talent/New York Kids
276 Fifth Avenue, Ste. 204
New York, NY 10001
(212) 532-6005

**Silver, Massetti & Szatmary/
East Ltd.**
145 West 45th Street, #1204
New York, NY 10036
(212) 391-4545

Ann Steele Agency
240 West 44th Street, Ste. 1
Helen Hayes Theatre
New York, NY 10036
(212) 278-0896

Peter Strain & Assoc., Inc.
1501 Broadway, #2900
New York, NY 10036
(212) 391-0380

Talent Network Group (TNG)
111 East 22nd Street, 3rd Fl.
New York, NY 10010
(212) 995-7325

Talent Representative, Inc.
20 East 53rd Street, Ste. 2A
New York, NY 10022
(212) 752-1835

Tamar Wolbrom, Inc.
130 West 42nd Street, Ste. 707
New York, NY 10036
(212) 398-4595

The Tantleff Office
375 Greenwich Street, Ste. 603
New York, NY 10013
(212) 941-3939

Tranum, Robertson & Hughes
600 Madison Avenue
New York, NY 10017
(212) 371-7500

Universal Attractions Inc.
225 West 57th Street
New York, NY 10019
(212) 582-7575

Waters Agency
1501 Broadway, #1305
New York, NY 10036
(212) 302-8787

Gail Williams Agency
525 South 4th Street, #364
Philadelphia, PA 19147
(215) 627-9533

Ann Wright Representatives
165 West 46th Street, #1105
New York, NY 10036
(212) 764-6770

Writers & Artists Agency
19 West 44th Street, #1000
New York, NY 10036
(212) 391-1112

LOS ANGELES

5 Star Talent Agency
2312 Janet Lee Drive
La Crescenta, CA 91214
(818) 249-4241

Ablaze Entertainment, Inc.
5155 Rosecrans Avenue, #1077
Los Angeles, CA 90250
(323) 871-2202

Abrams Artists Agency
9200 Sunset Boulevard, #1130
Los Angeles, CA 90069
(310) 859-0625

Abrams-Rubaloff & Lawrence
8075 West Third, #303
Los Angeles, CA 90048
(213) 935-1700

Acme Talent & Literary
4727 Wilshire Boulevard, #333
Los Angeles, CA 90010
(323) 954-2263

The Agency
1800 Avenue of the Stars, #400
Los Angeles, CA 90067
(310) 551-3000

**Agency for the
Performing Arts, Inc.**
9200 Sunset Boulevard, 9th Fl.
Los Angeles, CA 90069
(310) 273-0744

Agency West Entertainment
(formally J.E.O.W. Entertainment)
6255 West Sunset Boulevard, #908
Hollywood, CA 90028
(323) 468-9470

Aimee Entertainment Assoc.
15840 Ventura Boulevard, #215
Encino, CA 91436
(818) 783-9115

AKA Talent Agency
6310 San Vincente Boulevard
Los Angeles, CA 90048
(323) 965-5600

Allen Talent Agency
P.O. Box 1498
Los Angeles, CA 90078
(213) 605-1110

Alvarado Rey Agency
8455 Beverly Boulevard, Ste. 406
Los Angeles, CA 90048
(213) 655-7978

Amsel, Eisentstadt & Frazier, Inc.
5757 Wilshire Boulevard, Ste. 510
Los Angeles, CA 90036
(323) 939-1188

Angel City Talent
1680 Vine Street, #716
Hollywood, CA 90028
(323) 650-6885

Artists Agency
1180 South Beverly Drive, # 301
Los Angeles, CA 90035
(310) 277-7779

Artists Group, Ltd.
10100 Santa Monica Boulevard,
#2490
Los Angeles, CA 90067
(310) 552-1100

A.S.A.
4430 Fountain Avenue, #A
Hollywood, CA 90029
(323) 662-9787

Atkins & Associates
303 South Crescent Heights
Boulevard
Los Angeles, CA 90048
(323) 658-1025

The Austin Agency
6715 Hollywood Boulevard, #204
Hollywood, CA 90028
(323) 957-4444

Badgley & Connor, Inc.
9229 Sunset Boulevard, #311
Los Angeles, CA 90069
(310) 278-9313

Baier/Kleinman International
3575 Cahuenga Boulevard West, #500
Los Angeles, CA 90068
(818) 761-1001

Baldwin Talent, Inc.
8055 West Manchester Avenue
Playa del Rey, CA 90292
(310) 827-2422

Bobby Ball Talent Agency
4342 Lankershim Boulevard,
Universal City, CA 91602
(818) 506-8188

Baron Entertainment
5757 Wilshire Boulevard, Ste. 659
Los Angeles, CA 90036
(323) 936-7600

Bauman Redanty & Shaul
5757 Wilshire Boulevard, #473
Los Angeles, CA 90036
(323) 857-6666

Marian Berzon Agency
336 East 17th Street
Costa Mesa, CA 92627
(714) 631-5936

Bonnie Black Talent Agency
5318 Wilkinson, #A
Valley Village, CA 91607
(818) 753-5424

The Blake Agency
1333 Ocean Avenue
Santa Monica, CA 90401
(310) 899-9898

Brand Model & Talent Agency
1520 Brookhollow Drive, #39
Santa Ana, CA 92705
(714) 850-1158

The Brandt Company
15250 Ventura Boulevard, #720
Sherman Oaks, CA 91403
(818) 783-7747

Bresler Kelly & Associates
11500 West Olympic Boulevard, #510
Los Angeles, CA 90064
(310) 479-5611

Don Buchwald
& Assoc., Inc. Pacific
6500 Wilshire Boulevard, 22nd Fl.
Los Angeles, CA 90048
(323) 655-7400

Buchwald Talent Group, Inc.
A Youth Agency
Commercial Department
6300 Wilshire Boulevard, Ste. 910
Los Angeles, CA 90048
323-852-9555
Theatrical Department
6500 Wilshire Boulevard, Ste. 2210
Los Angeles, CA 90048
323-852-9559

Burton Agency, Inc., Iris
1450 Belfast Dr.
Los Angeles, CA 90069
(310) 288-0121

Barbara Cameron & Assoc., Inc.
8369 Sausalito Avenue, #A
West Hills, CA 91304
(818) 888-6107

Career Artists International
11030 Ventura Boulevard, #3
Studio City, CA 91604
(818) 980-1315

Cassell-Levy, Inc.
843 North Sycamore
Los Angeles, CA 90038
(323) 461-3971

Castle Hill Enterprises
1101 South Orlando Avenue
Los Angeles, CA 90035
(323) 653-3535

Cavaleri & Associates
178 South Victory Boulevard, #205
Burbank, CA 91506
(818) 955-9300

Champagne/Trott Agency
9250 Wilshire Boulevard #303
Beverly Hills, CA 90212
(310) 275-0067

The Charles Agency
11950 Ventura Boulevard, Ste. A
Studio City, CA 91604
(818) 761-2224

The Chasin Agency
8899 Beverly Boulevard, #716
Los Angeles, CA 90048
(310) 278-7505

Chateau Billings Talent Agency
5657 Wilshire Boulevard, #340
Los Angeles, CA 90036
(323) 965-5432

The Tory Christopher Group
6381 Hollywood Boulevard, Ste. 600
Hollywood, CA 90028
(323) 469-6906

Cinema Talent Agency
2609 Wyoming Avenue, Ste. A
Burbank, CA 91505
(818) 845-3816

Circle Talent Associates
433 North Camden Dr., #400
Beverly Hills, CA 90210
(310) 285-1585

W. Randolph Clark Co.
13415 Ventura Boulevard #3
Sherman Oaks, CA 91423
(818) 385-0583

Coleen Cler Talent Agency
178 South Victory Boulevard #108
Burbank, CA 91502
(818) 841-7943

Coast to Coast Talent Group, Inc.
3350 Barham Boulevard
North Hollywood, CA 90068
(323) 845-9200

Colours Model & Talent Mgmt
8344 1/2 West 3rd Street
Los Angeles, CA 90048
(213) 658-7072

Commercials Unlimited
8383 Wilshire Boulevard, #850
Beverly Hills, CA 90211
(323) 655-0069

Commercial Talent
9157 Sunset Boulevard #215
Los Angeles, CA 90069
(310) 247-1431

Contemporary Artists, Ltd.
1317 5th Street, #200
Santa Monica, CA 90401-2210
(310) 395-1800

The Coppage Company
5411 Camelia Avenue
North Hollywood, CA 91601
(818) 980-8806

JR Coralie Theatrical Agency
4789 Vineland Avenue, #100
North Hollywood, CA 91602
(818) 766-9501

Creative Artists
9830 Wilshire Boulevard
Beverly Hills, CA 90212
(310) 288-4545

The Crofoot Group, Inc.
23632 Calabasas Road, Ste. 104
Calabasas, CA 91302
(818) 223-1500

Culbertson-Argazzi Group
8430 Santa Monica Boulevard, #210
West Hollywood, CA 90069
(323) 650-9454

Cunningham Escott, Dipene & Assoc., Inc.
10635 Santa Monica Boulevard, #130
Los Angeles, CA 90025
(310) 475-2111

D.H. Talent
1800 North Highland, #300
Los Angeles, CA 90028
(323) 962-6643

Diverse Talent Group
1875 Century Park East #2250
Los Angeles, CA 90067
(310) 201-6565

Craig Dorfman & Asssociates
9200 Sunset Boulevard, #800
Los Angeles, CA 90069
(310) 858-1090

EBS/Los Angeles
3000 West Olympic Boulevard, #2438
Santa Monica, CA 90404
310-229-5989

Elle Chante Talent Agency
231 West 75th Street
Los Angeles, CA 90003
(323) 750-9490

The Endeavor Agency, LLC
9701 Wilshire Boulevard, 10th Fl.
Beverly Hills, CA 90212
(310) 248-2000

Epstein – Wyckoff – Corsa – Ross & Assoc.
280 South Beverly Drive, #400
Beverly Hills, CA 90212
(310) 278-7222

Evolve Talent Agency
3435 Wilshire Boulevard, Ste. 2700
Los Angeles, CA 90010
(213) 251-1734

Ferrar Media Associates
8430 Santa Monica Boulevard, #220
Los Angeles, CA 90069
(323) 654-2601

Film Artists Assoc.
4717 Van Nuys Boulevard, Ste. 215
Sherman Oaks, CA 91403
(818) 386-9669

Flick East – West Talent, Inc.
9057 Nemo Street
West Hollywood, CA 90069
(310) 271-9111

Judith Fontaine Agency
205 South Beverly Drive, #212
Beverly Hills, CA 90212
(310) 471-8631

Gwyn Foxx Talent Agency
6269 Selma Avenue, #18
Los Angeles, CA 90028
(323) 467-7711

Barry Freed Company
2040 Avenue of the Stars, #400
Los Angeles, CA 90067
(310) 277-1260

Alice Fries Agency
1927 Vista Del Mar Avenue
Los Angeles, CA 90068
(323) 464-1404

Gage Group, Inc.
9255 Sunset Boulevard, #515
Los Angeles, CA 90069
(310) 859-8777

Dale Garrick International
8831 Sunset Boulevard, #402
Los Angeles, CA 90069
(310) 657-2661

Geddes Agency
8430 Santa Monica Boulevard, #200
West Hollywood, CA 90069
323-848-2700

Laya Gelff Associates
16133 Ventura Boulevard, #700
Encino, CA 91436
(818) 996-3100

Phil Agency Inc.
232 North Canon Drive, #202
Beverly Hills, CA 90210
(310) 274-6611

Gold, Marshak, Liedtke & Assoc.
3500 West Olive, #1400
Burbank, CA 91505
(818) 972-4300

Michelle Gordon & Assoc.
260 South Beverly Drive, #308
Beverly Hills, CA 90212
(310) 246-9930

**Grant, Savic, Kopaloff
& Associates**
6399 Wilshire Boulevard, Ste. 414
Los Angeles, CA 90048
(323) 782-1854

Greene & Associates
526 North Larchmont Boulevard, #201
Los Angeles, CA 90004
(323) 960-1333

GVA Talent Agency, Inc.
9229 Sunset Boulevard, #320
Los Angeles, CA 90069
310-278-1310

Buzz Halliday & Associates
8899 Beverly Boulevard, #715
Los Angeles, CA 90048
(310) 275-6028

Halpern & Assoc.
12304 Santa Monica Boulevard, #104
Los Angeles, CA 90025
(310) 571-4488

Mitchell J. Hamilburg Agency
8671 Wilshire Boulevard #500
Beverly Hills, CA 90211
(310) 657-1501

Vaughn D. Hart & Assoc.
8899 Beverly Boulevard, #815
Los Angeles, CA 90048
(310) 273-7887

Beverly Hecht Agency
12001 Ventura Place, #320
Studio City, CA 91604-2626
(310) 505-1192

Hervey-Grims Talent Agency, Inc.
10561 Missouri, #1
Los Angeles, CA 90025
(323) 475-2010

Hilltop Talent Agency
27520 Hawthorne Boulevard, #133
Rolling Hills Estates, CA 90274
(310) 265-0611

Hollander Talent Group
3518 Caheunga Boulevard, Ste. 316
Los Angeles, CA 90068
(323) 845-4160

House of Representatives Talent
400 South Beverly , #101
Beverly Hills, CA 90212
(310) 772-0772

Howard Talent West
11374 Ventura Boulevard
Studio City, CA 91604
(818) 766-5300

HWA Talent Representatives
3500 West Olive Avenue, #1400
Burbank, CA 91505
(818) 972-4310

IFA Talent Agency
8730 Sunset Boulevard, #490
West Hollywood, CA 90069
(310) 659-5522

Innovative Artists Commercial & Voiceover, Inc.
1505 Tenth Street
Santa Monica, CA 90401
(310) 656-0400

Innovative Artists Talent & Literary Agency
3000 Olympic Boulevard,
Bldg. 4, Ste. 1200
Santa Monica, CA 90404
(310) 553-5200

Innovative Artists Young Talent Division
3000 Olympic Boulevard,
Bldg. 4, Ste. 1200
Santa Monica, CA 90404
(310) 553-5200

International Creative Mgmt. (I.C.M.)
8942 Wilshire Boulevard
Beverly Hills, CA 90211
(310) 550-4000

Kaplan-Stahler Agency
8383 Wilshire Boulevard, #923
Beverly Hills, CA 90211
(310) 653-4483

Kazarian-Spencer & Assoc., Inc.
11365 Ventura Boulevard, #100
Studio City, 91604
(818) 769-9111

William Kerwin Agency
1605 North Cahuenga, #202
Hollywood, CA 90028
(323) 469-5155

Eric Klass Agency
139 South Beverly Drive, #331
Beverly Hills, CA 90212
(310) 274-9169

KM & Associates
4922 Vineland Avenue
North Hollywood, CA 91601
(818) 766-3566

Paul Kohner, Inc.
9300 Wilshire Boulevard, #555
Beverly Hills, CA 90212
(310) 550-1060

L.A. Talent, Inc.
7700 West Sunset Boulevard
Los Angeles, CA 90046
(323) 656-3722

Stacey Lane Agency
1085 Carolyn Way
Beverly Hills, CA 90210
(818) 501-2668

Sid Levin Talent Agency
8484 Wilshire Boulevard, #750
Beverly Hills, CA 90211
(323) 653-7073

Lichtman/Salners Company
12216 Moorpark Street
Studio City, CA 91604
(818) 655-9898

Robert Light Agency
6404 Wilshire Boulevard, #900
Los Angeles, CA 90048
(323) 651-1777

Ken Lindner & Assoc.
2049 Century Park East, #3050
Los Angeles, CA 90067
(310) 277-9223

LJ & Associates
17328 Ventura Boulevard, #185
Encino, CA 91316
(818) 589-6960

Lovell & Assoc.
6730 Wedgewood Place
Los Angeles, CA 90068
(323) 876-1560

Jana Luker Agency
1923 1/2 Westwood Boulevard, #3
Los Angeles, CA 90025
(310) 441-2822

Lynne & Reilly Agency
10725 Vanowen Street, #113
North Hollywood, CA 91605-6402
(213) 755-6434

McCabe/Justice, LLC
247 South Beverly, #102
Beverly Hills, CA 90212
(310) 274-7815

McDonald/Selznick Associates, Inc.
1611A North El Centro Avenue
Hollywood, CA 90028
(323) 957-6680

Malaky International
10642 Santa Monica Boulevard, #103
Los Angeles, CA 90025
(310) 234-9114

Maris Agency
17620 Sherman Way, #213
Van Nuys, CA 91406
(818) 708-2493

Alese Marshall Model & Talent
22730 Hawthorne Boulevard, #201
Torrance, CA 90505
(310) 378-1223

Maxine's Talent Agency
4830 Encino Ave
Encino, CA 91316
(818) 986-2946

Media Artists Group
6404 Wilshire Boulevard, Ste. 950
Los Angeles, CA 90048
(323) 658-5050

Meridian Artists Agency
9229 Sunset Boulevard, #310
Los Angeles, CA 90069
(310) 246-2611

Metropolitan Talent Agency
4526 Wilshire Boulevard
Los Angeles, CA 90010
(323) 857-4500

**Models Guild of California
Talent Agency**
8489 West 3rd Street, #1107
Los Angeles, CA 90048
(323) 801-2132

The Morgan Agency
129 West Wilson Street, #202
Costa Mesa, CA 92627
(714) 574-1120

William Morris Agency, Inc.
151 El Camino
Beverly Hills, CA 90212
(310) 274-7451

David Moss & Assoc.
733 North Seward Street, P.H.
Los Angeles, CA 90038
(323) 465-1234

Susan Nathe & Assoc. (CPC)
8281 Melrose, #200
Los Angeles, CA 90046
(323) 653-7573

Omnipop, Inc.
10700 Ventura Boulevard, 2nd Fl.
Studio City, CA 91604
(818) 980-9267

The Orange Grove Group, Inc.
12178 Ventura Boulevard, #205
Studio City, CA 91604
(818) 762-7498

Origin Talent
3393 Barham Boulevard
Los Angeles, CA 90068
(323) 845-4141

Cindy Osbrink Talent Agency
4343 Lankershim Boulevard, #100
Universal City, CA 91602
(818) 760-2488

Pakula/King & Associates
9229 Sunset Boulevard, #315
Los Angeles, CA 90069
(310) 281-4868

**Paradigm,
A Talent & Literary Agency**
10100 Santa Monica Boulevard,
#2500
Los Angeles, CA 90067
(310) 277-4400

The Paradise Group
8749 Sunset Boulevard, Ste. B
Los Angeles, CA 90069
(310) 854-6622

Pinnacle Commercial Talent
5757 Wilshire Boulevard, Ste. 510
Los Angeles, CA 90036
(323) 939-1188

Playboy Model Agency
9242 Beverly Boulevard
Beverly Hills, CA 90210
(310) 246-4000

Privelege Talent Agency
9229 Sunset Boulevard, #414
West Hollywood, CA 90069
(310) 858-5277

Progressive Artists
400 South Beverly, #216
Beverly Hills, CA 90212
(310) 553-8561

Qualita Dell'Arte
5353 Topanga Canyon Road, Ste. 220
Woodland Hills, CA 91364
(818) 340-9249

Sarnoff Company, Inc.
3500 West Olive Avenue, Ste. 300
Burbank, CA 91505
(818) 973-4555

Savage Agency, Inc.
6212 Banner Avenue
Los Angeles, CA 90038
(213) 461-8316

Jack Scagnetti Agency
5118 Vineland Avenue, #102
North Hollywood, CA 91601
(818) 762-3871

Irv Schechter Company
9300 Wilshire Boulevard, #400
Beverly Hills, CA 90212
(310) 278-8070

Sandie Schnarr Talent, Inc.
8500 Melrose Avenue, #212
West Hollywood, Ca 90069
(310) 360-7680

Judy Schoen & Assoc.
606 North Larchmont Boulevard,
#309
Los Angeles, CA 90004
(323) 962-1950

Screen Artists Agency
4526 Sherman Oaks Avenue
Sherman Oaks, CA 91403
(818) 789-4897

SDB Partners, Inc.
1801 Avenue of the Stars, #902
Los Angeles, CA 90067
(310) 785-0060

David Shapira & Assoc., Inc.
15821 Ventura Boulevard, #235
Encino, CA 91436
(818) 906-0322

Shapiro-Lichtman Stein
8827 Beverly Boulevard
Los Angeles, CA 90048
(310) 859-8877

Shumaker Agency
6533 Hollywood Boulevard, #401
Hollywood, CA 90028
(323) 464-0745

**Silver, Massetti & Szatmary/
West, Ltd.**
3870 Sunset Boulevard, #440
Los Angeles, CA 90069
(310) 289-0909

Michael Slessinger & Assoc.
8730 Sunset Boulevard, Ste. 270
West Hollywood, CA 90069
(310) 657-7113

Camille Sorice Talent Agency
13412 Moorpark Street, #C
Sherman Oaks, CA 91423
(818) 955-1775

Special Artists Agency
345 North Maple Drive, #302
Beverly Hills, CA 90210
(310) 859-9688

Scott Stander Agency
13701 Riverside Drive, Ste. 201
Sherman Oaks, CA 91423
(818) 905-7000

Starcraft Agency
3330 Barham Boulevard, #105
Los Angeles, CA 90068
(323) 845-4784

The Stevens Group
3518 Cahuenga Boulevard,
West #306
Los Angeles, CA 90068
(323) 850-5761

Stone Manners
8436 West 3rd Street, #740
Los Angeles, CA 90048
(323) 655-1313

Peter Strain & Assoc.
5724 West 3rd Street, # 302
Los Angeles, CA 90036
(323) 525-3391

Mitchell K. Stubbs & Associates
8675 West Washington Boulevard,
#203
Culver City, CA 90232
(310) 888-1200

Superior Talent Agency
11425 Moorpark Street
Studio City, CA 91602
(818) 508-5627

Sutton-Barth-Vennari, Inc.
145 South Fairfax Avenue, #310
Los Angeles, CA 90036
(323) 938-6000

SWB Theatrical
8383 Wilshire Boulevard, #850
Beverly Hills, CA 90211
(323) 655-0069

Talent Group, Inc.
6300 Wilshire Boulevard, #900
Los Angeles, CA 90048
(323) 852-9559

Herb Tannen & Assoc.
10801 National Boulevard, #101
Los Angeles, CA 90064
(310) 466-5822

Thomas Talent Agency
6709 LaTijera, #915
Los Angeles, CA 90045
(310) 665-0000

Arlene Thornton & Assoc.
12001 Ventura Boulevard, #201
Studio City, CA 91604-2609
(818) 760-6688

Tisherman Agency
6767 Forest Lawn Drive, #101
Los Angeles, CA 90068
(323) 850-6767

Two Angels Agency
2026 Cliff Drive, Ste. 200
Santa Barbara, A 93109
(805) 957-9654

United Artists Talent Agency
14011 Ventura Boulevard, #213
Sherman Oaks. CA 91423
(818) 788-7305

United Talent Agency
9560 Wilshire Boulevard
Beverly Hills, CA 90212
(310)-273-6700

The Vission Agency
1801 Century Park East, 24th Fl.
Los Angeles, CA 90067
(310) 553-8833

Vox, Inc.
6300 Wilshire Boulevard, Ste. 900
Los Angeles, CA 90048
(323) 852-9559

The Wallis Agency
4444 Riverside Drive, #105
Burbank, CA 91505
(818) 953-4848

Wardlow & Assoc.
(Formerly Camden)
1501 Main Street, #204
Venice, CA 90291
(310) 452-1292

Waters & Nicolosi
9301 Wilshire Boulevard, #300
Beverly Hills, CA 90210
(310) 777-8277

Ann Waugh Agency
4741 Laurel Canyon Boulevard,
Ste 200
North Hollywood, CA 91607
(818) 980-0141

Shirley Wilson & Assoc.
5410 Wilshire Boulevard, Ste. 806
Los Angeles, CA 90036
(323) 857-6977

Writers & Artists Agency
8383 Wilshire Boulevard, #550
Los Angeles, CA 90211
(323) 866-0900

Zadeh & Assoc.
5435 Balboa Boulevard, #212
Encino, CA 91316
818-501-0800

Zanuck, Passon & Pace, Inc.
4717 Van Nuys Boulevard, Ste. 102
Sherman Oaks, CA 94103
(818) 783-4890

CHICAGO

Ambassador Talent Agents, Inc.
333 North Michigan Avenue, #910
Chicago, IL 60601
(312) 641-3491

Aria Model & Talent Mgmt., LLC
1017 West Washington Street, Ste. 2C
Chicago, IL 60607
(312) 243-9400

**Baker & Rowley
Talent Agency, Inc.**
1327 West Washington Boulevard,
Ste. 5C
Chicago, IL 60607
(312) 850-4700

Best Impressions Agency, Inc.
477 East Butterfield Road, #302
Lombard, IL 60148
(630) 434-2214

Big Mouth Talent Agency
935 West Chestnut, Ste. 415
Chicago, IL 60622
(312) 421-4400

The Emmrich Agency
18622 Brook Forest Avenue,
Street Rt. 59
Shorewood, IL 60431
(815) 577-8650

Encore Talent Agency, Inc.
700 North Sacramento Boulevard,
Ste. 231
Chicago, IL 60612
(773) 638-7300

ETA, Inc.
7558 South Chicago Avenue
Chicago, IL 60619
(312) 752-3955

Ford Talent Group
641 West Lake Street, Ste. 402
Chicago, IL 60661
(312) 707-9000

Geddes Agency
1633 North Halsted Street, #400
Chicago, IL 60614
(312) 787-8333

Shirley Hamilton Inc.
333 East Ontario Street, Ste. B
Chicago, IL 60611
(312) 787-4700

Linda Jack Talent
230 East Ohio Street, #200
Chicago, IL 60611
(312) 587-1155

Jennifer's Talent Unlimited, Inc.
740 North Plankinton Street, Ste. 300
Milwaukee, Wisconsin 53203-2403
(414) 277-9440

Lily's Talent Agency
1301 West Washington Street, Ste. B
Chicago, IL 60607
(312) 601-2345

Lori Lins Ltd.
7611 West Holmes Avenue
Greenfield, WI 53220
(414) 282-3500

Naked Voices, Inc.
865 North Sangamon Street, Ste. 415
Chicago, IL 60622
(312) 563-0136

Salazar & Navas Inc.
760 North Odgen Street, #2200
Chicago, IL 60622
(312) 666-1677

Norman Schucart Enterprises
1417 Green Bay Road
Highland Park, IL 60035
(708) 433-1113

Stewart Talent Mgmt., Corp.
58 West Huron Street
Chicago, IL 60610
(312) 943-3131

Voices Unlimited Inc.
541 North Fairbanks Street, Ste. 2735
Chicago, IL 60611
(312) 832-1113

Arlene Wilson Talent, Inc.
430 West Erie Street, Ste. 210
Chicago, IL 60610
(312) 573-0200

Arlene Wilson Talent, Inc.
807 North Jefferson Street, 200
Milwaukee, WI 53202
(414) 283-5600

Casting Directors

NEW YORK

AAAVoiceCasting
123 West 18th Street, 7th Fl.
New York, NY 10011
(212) 675-3240
e-mail: AAAVoiceCasting@aol.com

Amerifilm Casting, Inc.
c/o Silvercup Studios
42-22 22nd Street, Room M-104
Long Island City, New York 11101
(646) 498-6252

Background, Inc.
20 West 20th Street, Ste. 234
New York, NY 10011
(212) 6o09-1103
Web site: www.bgroundinc.com

Bradley Barro
P.O. Box 1023
Fort Lee, NJ 07024
(201) 313-1107

Bass-Visgilio Casting
648 Broadway, #912
New York, NY 10012
(212) 598-9032

Jerry Beaver & Associates Casting
215 Park Avenue South, Ste. 1704
New York, NY 10003
(212) 979-0909

Breanna Benjamin Casting
PO Box 21077-PACC
New York, NY 10129
(212) 388-2347

Jay Binder Casting
321 West 44th Street, Ste. 606
New York, NY 10036

Block Casting
Box 170, 16710 First Avenue
New York, NY 10128
(212) 348-8371
e-mail: block__casting@hotmail.com

Blue Man Productions
599 Broadway, 5th Fl.
New York, NY 10012
(212) 226-6366
e-mail: casting@blueman.com
Web site: www.blueman.com

Nora Brennan Casting
752 West End Avenue, Ste. Mezz C
New York, NY 10025
(212) 531-1825

Kristine Bulakowski Casting
Prince Street Station, P.O. Box 616
New York, NY 10012
(212) 769-8550

James Calleri
630 Ninth Avenue, Ste. 708
New York, NY 10036
(212) 564-1235

Donald Case Casting Inc.
386 Park Avenue South, Ste. 809
New York, NY 10016
(212) 889-6555

The Casting Connection
Ste. 2A, Central Square
199 New Road
Linwood, NJ 08221
Talent Hot Line: (609) 601-CAST
Fax: (609) 926-6219

Casting Solutions
231 West 29th Street, Ste. 601
New York, NY 10001
(212) 875-7573

CBS Entertainment
207 West 25th Street, 6th Fl.
New York, NY 10001

Chantiles Vignealt Casting, Inc.
39 West 19th Street, 12th Fl.
New York, NY 10011

Ellen Chenoweth, C.S.Q.
c/o C.S.A.
145 West 28th Street, Ste. 12-F
New York, NY 10001

Roz Clancy Casting
76 Wilfred Avenue
Washington Crossing, NJ 08560
(609) 730-1090 (24-hour hotline)

Rich Cole
648 Broadway, Ste. 912
New York, NY 10012
(212) 614-7130

Jodi Collins Casting
853 Broadway, Ste. #803
New York, NY 10003
Client line: (212) 254-3400
Client Fax: 254-2559
Talent Fax: 982-1086
(business hours only)

Complete Casting
(212) 265-7460

Byron Crystal
41 Union Square West, Ste. 316
New York, NY 10003

Sue Crystal Casting
251 West 87th Street, #26
New York, NY 10024
(212) 877-0737

CTP Casting
207 West 25th Street, 6th Fl.
New York, NY 10001

**Merry L. Delmonte
Casting & Productions, Inc.**
575 Madison Avenue
New York, NY 10022

Donna DeSeta Casting
525 Broadway, 3rd Fl.
New York, NY 10012

Joan D'Incecco Casting
Fax: (201) 265-6016

Pennie Du Pont
36 Perry Street
New York, NY 10014

Sylvia Fay
71 Park Avenue
New York, NY 10016

Linda Ferrara Casting
217 East 86th Street, Ste. 188
New York, NY 10028

Alan Filderman Casting
333 West 39th Street, #601A
New York, NY 10018
(212) 695-6200

Leonard Finger
1501 Broadway
New York, NY 10036

Denise Fitzgerald Casting
284 Lafayette Street, Ste. 1C
New York, NY 10012
e-mail: Dfcast@usa.net

Judie Fixler Casting
P.O. Box 149
Green Farms, CT 06436-0149
(203) 254-4416

Janet Foster
3212 Cambridge Avenue
Riverdale, NY 10463

Gilburne & Urban Casting
80 Varick Street, Ste. 6A
New York, NY 10013
(212) 965-0745

Godlove & Company Casting
151 West 25th Street, 11th Fl.
New York, NY 10001
(212) 627-7300

Amy Gossels Casting
1382 Third Avenue
New York, NY 10021
(212)472-6981

Maria & Tony Greco Casting
(Dovetail Entertainment)
630 Ninth Avenue, No. 702
New York, NY 10036

Joey Guastella Casting
85-10 151st Avenue, #5B
Queens, NY 11414
(718) 835-6451

Jimmy Hank Promotions
209 West 104th Street, Ste. 2H
New York, NY 10025
(212) 864-2132
e-mail: TVEXEC4U@aol.com

Carol Hanzel Casting
48 West 21st Street, 7th Fl.
New York, NY 10010
(212) 242-6113

**Judy Henderson &
Associates Casting**
330 West 89th Street
New York, NY 10024
(212) 877-0225

Herman & Lipson Casting, Inc.
24 West 25th Street
New York, NY 10010

Stuart Howard Associates, Ltd.
207 West 25th Street, 6th Fl.
New York, NY 10001
(212) 725-7770

Hughes Moss Casting Ltd.
1600 Broadway, Ste. 705A
New York, NY 10019-7413
(212) 307-6690

Impossible Casting
122 West 26th Street, 11th Fl.
New York, NY 10001
(212) 255-3029

Kalin/Todd Casting
425 East 58th Street, Ste. 4D
New York, NY 10022
(212) 585-1766

Avy Kaufman
180 Varick Street, 16th Fl.
New York, NY 10014

Kee Casting
234 Fifth Avenue
New York, NY 10001
(212) 725-3775

Judy Keller Casting
140 West 22nd Street, 4th Fl.
New York, NY 10011

Kipperman Casting, Inc.
12 West 37th Street, 3rd Fl.
New York, NY 10018

Stephanie Klapper Casting
41 West 86th Street, Ste. 3D
New York, NY 10024
(212) 580-0688
Fax: (212) 769-3177

Andrea Kurzman Casting Inc.
122 East 37th Street, 2nd Fl.
New York, NY 10016
(212) 684-0710

Lelas Talent Casting
P.O. Box 128
Guilford, CT 06437
(203) 457-2223

Mike Lemon Casting, C.S.A.
413 North 7th Street, Ste. 602
Philadelphia, PA 19123
(215) 627-8927
Talent Hotline: (215) 627-1574
e-mail:
micmail@mikelemoncasting.com
Web site: www.mikelemoncasting.com

Liz Lewis Casting Partners
129 West 20th Street
New York, NY 10011
(212) 645-1500

Liebhart/Alberg Casting
1710 First Avenue, #122
New York, NY 10128

Joan Lynn Casting
39 West 19th Street, 12th Fl.
New York, NY 10011
(212) 675-5595

Mackey/Sandrich Casting, C.S.A.
c/o C.S.A.
145 West 28th Street, Ste. 12-F
New York, NY 10001
(212) 982-5900

Joel Manaloto Casting
1480 York Avenue, Fourth Fl.
New York, NY 10021
(212) 517-3737

Mindy Marin
Bluewater Ranch Entertainment, Inc.
Casting Artists, Inc.
451 Greenwich Street, 7th Fl.
New York, NY 10013

McCorkle Casting, Ltd.
264 West 40th Street, 9th Fl.
New York, NY 10018
(212) 840-0992

Abigail McGrath, Inc.
484 West 43rd Street, Ste. 37-S
New York, NY 10036

McHale Barone
30 Irving Place, 6th Fl.
New York, NY 10003

Beth Melsky
928 Broadway
New York, NY 10010
(212) 505-5000

Norman Meranus Casting
201 West 85th Street, 16-D
New York, NY 10024

Matthew Messinger
c/o No Soap Productions
1600 Broadway, Ste. 407
New York, NY 10019

Jeff Mitchell Casting
440 Park Avenue South, 11th Fl.
New York, NY 10016
(212) 679-3550

MTV Talent
1515 Broadway, 25th Fl.
New York, NY 10036

Mungioli Theatricals, Inc.
207 West 25th Street, 6th Fl.
New York, NY 10001
(212) 337-8832

Elissa Myers, Inc.
333 West 52nd Street, Ste. 1008
New York, NY 10019

Navarro/Bertoni & Associates
101 West 31st Street, Room 1707
New York, NY 10001

Nickelodeon
1515 Broadway, 38th Fl.
New York, NY 10036

Steven O'Neill
VP of Casting – NBC
30 Rockefeller Plaza, Room 1265E
New York, NY 10112

Orpheus Group
1600 Broadway, Ste. 410
New York, NY 10019
(212) 957-8760

Michele Ortlip Casting
(508) 696-0944
Fax: (508) 696-3111
e-mail: ortlipcasting@cs.com

Joanne Pasciuto Inc.
17-08 150th Street
Whitestone, NY 11357

The Philadelphia Casting Co., Inc.
128 Chestnut Street, Ste. 403
Philadelphia, PA 19106
Producers, Directors, Agents:
(215) 592-7575
Number for actors only:
(215) 592-7577
e-mail: Casting@Philacast.com
Do not e-mail or fax pictures

Eileen Powers Casting (EPC)
8 Fulton Drive
Brewster, NY 10509
(845) 279-5106

Michele Pulice Casting
Website:
www.michelepulicecasting.com

Laura Richin Casting
33 Douglass Street, Ste. #1
Brooklyn, NY 11231
(718) 802-9628

Toni Roberts Casting, Ltd.
150 Fifth Avenue, Ste. 309
New York, NY 10011

Mike Roscoe Casting, Ltd.
Times Square Station, P.O. Box 721
New York, NY 10108-60721
(212) 627-8880

Charles Rosen Casting, Inc.
140 West 22nd Street, 4th Fl.
New York, NY 10011

Judy Rosensteel Casting
43 West 68th Street
New York, NY 10023

**Rossmon Casting and
Talent Relations**
35 West 36th Street, 8th Fl.
New York, NY 10018
(212) 279-9229

Cindi Rush Casting
c/o Momentum Productions
36 West 25th Street, 2nd Fl.
New York, NY 10010

Paul Russell Casting
347 West 36th Street, 12th Fl.
New York, NY 10018

Jennifer Low Sauer Casting
332 Bleecker Street, PMB #D-8
New York, NY 10014
Website:
www.JennifrereLowSauerCasting
.homestead.com

**Howard Schwartz
Recording/HSR NY**
420 Lexington Avenue, Ste. 1934
New York, NY 10170
(212) 687-4180

Brien Scott
71-10 Loubet Street
Forest Hills, NY 11375
(718) 544-6902

Selective Casting by Carol Nadell
P.O. Box 1538
Radio City Station, NY 10101-1538

Shirley Sender
(917) 816-6888

Caroline Sinclair Casting
85 West Broadway
New York, NY 10007
(212) 566-0255

Winsome Sinclair & Associates
314 West 53rd Street, Ste. 106
New York, NY 10019
(212) 397-1537
e-mail: SINCO65@aol.com

Sirius Casting
29 John Street, PMB 126
New York, NY 10038
(917) 586-7497
e-mail: siriuscasting@aol.com

Skyrme, Lewis, & Fox Casting
459 Columbus Avenue, #164
New York, NY 10024
(212) 724-1121

Spotty Dog Productions
236 West 27th Street, 6th Fl.
New York, NY 10001
(212) 463-8550

Stark Naked Productions
39 West 19th Street, 12th Fl.
New York, NY 10011
(212) 366-1903

Adrienne Stern
149 Fifth Avenue, #730
New York, NY 10010
(212) 253-1496

Strickman-Ripps, Inc.
65 North Moore Street, Ste. 3A
New York, NY 10013
(212) 966-3211

Helyn Taylor Casting
140 West 58th Street
New York, NY 10019

T.E.C. Casting
2-15 26th Avenue
Long Island City, NY 11102

Bernard Telsey Casting
145 West 28th Street, 12th Fl.
New York, NY 10001
(212) 868-1260
Fax: (212) 868-1261

Todd Thaler Casting
130 West 57th Street, #10A
New York, NY 10019

Theatreworks/USA
151 West 26th Street, 7th Fl.
New York, NY 10001
(212) 647-1100

TNN (The National Network)
1515 Broadway, 38th Fl.
New York, NY 10036

Total Request Live
1515 Broadway, 23rd Fl.
New York, NY 10036

VH1
1633 Broadway, 6th Fl.
New York, NY 10019

VideoActive Talent
1780 Broadway, Studio 804
New York, NY 10019
(212) 541-8106
Websites: www.videoactiveprod.com
and www.joefrannklin.com
e-mail: vworks@aol.com

VoiceHunter.com
10 Sunset Drive
Weston, CT 06883
(800) 867-9532
Website: www.voicehunter.com

Warner Bros. Television Casting
1325 Avenue of the Americas,
32nd Fl.
New York, NY 10019
(212) 636-5145

Joy Weber Casting
c/o One on One
126 West 23rd Street
New York, NY 10011
(212) 206-0001

Kathy Wickline Casting
1080 North Delaware Avenue,
Ste. 100
Philadelphia, PA 19125
(215) 739-90952
Website: www.wicklinecasting.com

Grant Wilfley Casting
60 Madison Avenue, Room 1027
New York, NY 10010
(212) 685-3537

Marji Camner Wollin & Associates
233 East 69th Street
New York, NY 10021
(212) 472-2528

Liz Woodman Casting
11 Riverside Drive, #2JE
New York, NY 10023
(212) 787-3782

World Promotions
216 Crown Street, 5th Fl.
New Haven, CT 06510
(2034) 781-3427

LOS ANGELES

Melissa Abesera Casting
302 North La Brea, #71
Los Angeles, CA 90036
(323) 931-5622
Fax: (323) 931-1799
e-mail: abseracastinglaol.com
Web site: www.abseracasting.com

Cecily Adams Casting
CBS Studio Center
4024 Radford Avenue,
Bldg. 2, Rm. 102
Studio City, CA 91604
(818) 655-6092

Mercedes Alberti-Penney
175 East Olive Avenue, #402
Burbank, CA 90028
(323) 468-5010

Krisha Bullock Alexander
6230 Sunset Boulevard
Los Angeles, CA 90028
(323) 468-5010

Stacy Alexander
(See VH1)
(323) 752-8345

Johnny Almaraz
(323) 654-0273

Jill Anthony
(see Mossberg/Anthony Casting)

Deborah Aquila, C.S.A.
1041 North Formosa Avenue
Santa Monica Bldg., West #213
West Hollywood, CA 90046

Maureen Arata, C.S.A.
(See C.S.A.)

Nicole Arbusto
(See Dickson-Arbusto Casting)

Karen Armstrong
114 North Glendora Avenue, #227
Glendora, CA 91741
(909) 599-5838
e-mail: Karenj@clubnrt.net

Artz/Cohen Casting, C.S.A.
5225 Wilshire Boulevard, #624
Los Angeles, CA 90036
(323) 938-1043

ASG Casting, Inc., C.C.D.A.
10200 Riverside Drive, Ste. 205
Toluca Lake, CA 91602
(818) 762-0200

Julie Ashton Casting
10960 Wilshire Boulevard, 6th Fl.
Los Angeles, CA 90024
(310) 235-9320
Fax: (310) 235-9311

David Aulicino
(See Viacom Productions)

Pamela Azmi-Andrew
c/o Paramount Studios
Clara Bow Bldg., Rm. 117
Los Angeles, CA 90035
(323) 956-2621

Patrick Baca, C.S.A.
Nassif & Baca Casting
8306 Wilshire Boulevard, PMB #7004
Beverly Hills, CA 90211

Jeanie Bacharach Casting
10202 West Washington Boulevard
Culver City, CA 90232
(310) 369-3448

Rise Barish Casting, C.C.D.A.
21537 Pacific Coast Highway
Malibu, CA 90265
(310) 456-9018
(310) 458-1100

Carol Elizabeth Barlow Casting
7060 Hollywood Boulevard, Ste. 522
Hollywood, CA 90028

Anthony Barnao
c/o The Lex Theater
6760 Lexington Avenue
Los Angeles, CA 90038
(323) 663-7973

Matthew Barry, C.S.A.
4924 Balboa Boulevard, #371
Encino, CA 91316
(818) 759-4425

Deborah Barylski Casting, C.S.A.
(See C.S.A.)

Fran Bascom, C.S.A.
Columbia Pictures TV, Studio Plaza
3400 Riverside Drive, #765
Burbank, CA 91505
(818) 973-8339

Pamela Basker Casting
(818) 506-7348

Lisa Beach, C.S.A.
(See C.S.A., #311)
(323) 468-6633

Elyde Belasco
20th Century Fox
10201 West Pico Boulevard,
Bldg. 12, Rm. 201
Los Angeles, CA 90035

Belshe Casting
Long Beach Office: (562) 434-0550
Universal City Office: (818) 464-2718
e-mail: BelsheCasting@aol.com

Brett Benner
(See Romano/Benner Casting)

Annette Benson, C.S.A.
(See C.S.A.)

Terry Berland Casting, C.C.D.A.
(310) 571-4141
(See Westside Casting)

Amy Jo Berman
(310) 201-9537
(See HBO)

Chemin Bernard
Sunset/Gower Studios
1438 North Gower,
Bldg. 13, Room 206
Los Angeles, CA 90028
(323) 468-4858

Juel Bestrop
Jeanne McCarthy & Juel
Bestrop Casting
5225 Wilshire Boulevard, Ste. 418
Los Angeles, CA 90036
(323) 934-8363

Sharon Bialy, C.S.A.
P.O. Box 570308
Tarzana, CA 91356
(818) 342-8630
Fax: (818) 342-8744

Tammara Billik Casting, C.S.A.
13547 Ventura Boulevard, #688
Sherman Oaks, CA 91423

Joe Blake
(See Westside Casting)

Barbie Block
(See Sally Stiner Casting)

Susan Bluestein, C.S.A.
Universal Studios
100 Universal City Plaza, Trailer 6159
Universal City, CA 91608
(818) 6733-2666

Gene Blythe
(See Touchstone Television/ ABC
Entertainment)

Charlie Bogdan Casting
42 Smith Alley
Pasadena, CA 91103
(310) 399-7545
(626) 685-9515

Susan Booker
P.O. Box 2223
Malibu, CA 90265
(310) 457-5537

Deedee Bradley, C.S.A.
(See Warner Bros. TV)
(818) 954-7841

Eve Brandstein Casting
10880 Wilshire Boulevard, Ste. 1200
Los Angeles, CA 90024
(310) 234-2266

Megan Branman, C.S.A.
(See Warner Bros. TV)

Kate Brinegar, C.S.A.
Executive in Charge of
Talent & Casting
Fox Family Network
10960 Wilshire Boulevard, Ste. 1888
Los Angeles, CA 980024
(310) 235-9715
Fax: (310) 235-9560

Jackie Briskey, C.S.A.
4024 Radford Avenue,
Admin. Bldg., Ste. 280
Studio City, CA 91604
(818) 655-5601

Amy McIntyre Britt
c/o Buffy the Vampire Slayer
1800 Stewart Street
Santa Monica, CA 90404
(310) 579-5125
(See also CFB Casting)

Steve Brooksbank, C.S.A.
(See Slater/Brooksbank Casting)

Andrew Brown
(See Paramount Pictures Features
Casting)

Brown-West Casting
7319 Beverly Boulevard, #10
Los Angeles, CA 90036
(323) 938-2575

Mary V. Buck, C.S.A.
President, C.S.A.
(See Buck/EdelmanCasting)

Buck/Edelman Casting
4045 Radford Avenue, Ste. B
Studio City, CA 91604
(818) 506-7328

Buena Vista Motion
Picture Group
(Disney Feature Films, Touchstone
Pictures, Hollywood Pictures)
500 South Buena Vista Street
Burbank, CA 91521
(818) 560-7510

Perry Bullington, C.S.A.
(See MacDonald/Bullington Casting)

Burrows-Boland Casting
(310) 503-4719

Irene Cagen, C.S.A.
(See C.S.A.)
(323) 525-1381

Craig Campobasso, C.S.A.
(See C.S.A.)

Akua Campanella, C.S.A.
26730 Lacy Street
Los Angeles, CA 90031
(323) 222-1656
(212) 591-0945

Pamela Campus, C.C.D.A.
c/o Westside Casting Studios
2050 South Bundy Drive
Los Angeles, CA 90025
(818) 897-1588

Reuben Cannon
& Associates, C.S.A.
5225 Wilshire Boulevard, Ste. 526
Los Angeles, CA 90036
(323) 939-3190

Blythe Cappello
5225 Wilshire Boulevard, Ste. 418
Los Angeles, CA 90036
(323) 934-8363

Cathi Carlton, C.C.D.A.
(See Westside Casting)

Ferne Cassel, C.S.A.
(See C.S.A.)

Alice Cassidy, C.S.A.
(See C.S.A.)
Fax: (323) 931-4381

Cast of Thousands –
Lisa S. Beasley
P.O. Box 1687
Burbank, CA 91507
(818) 985-9995

The Casting Company
7461 Beverly Boulevard, Penthouse
Los Angeles, CA 90036
(323) 938-0700

The Casting Connection
1125 North Lindero Canyon Road
Ste. A8, Room 314
Westlake Village, CA 91362
LA Producers, Directors, Agents: (818)
991-2716

Casting Diva
1556 North La Brea Avenue, Ste. 100
Hollywood, CA 90028
(323) 465-3581

Casting Society
of America (C.S.A.)
606 North Larchmont Boulevard, 45B
Los Angeles, CA 90004
(323) 463-1925

Casting Works LA
902 East 5th Street
Austin, TX 78702
(512) 485-3113

Lucy Cavalo
(See CBS)

CBS
7800 Beverly Boulevard, #284
Los Angeles, CA 90036
(323) 575-2335

Central Union/ Central Non-Union
220 South Flower Street
Burbank, CA 91502
(818) 562-2700

Cervantes Casting
Toni Cervantes
Village Studio
519 Broadway
Santa Monica, CA 90401
(323) 954-0007

CFB Casting
Amy McIntyre Britt (310) 579-5125
Anya Colloff and Jennifer Fishman
Pate (323) 956-4701

Lindsay Chag
Living Dream Productions
4313 Bakman Avenue
Studio City, CA 91602
(818) 769-9576

Denise Chamian, C.S.A.
(See C.S.A.)

Fern Champion Casting
8255 Sunset Boulevard
Los Angeles, CA 90046
(323) 650-1280

Karen Church
(See CBS)

Barbara Claman, C.S.A.
5184 Canoga Avenue
Woodland Hills, CA 91365
(818) 704-1294

Lori Cobe-Ross
2005 Palo Verde Avenue, #306
Long Beach, CA 90815
(562) 938-9088

Andrea Cohen
4053 Radford Avenue, #109
Studio City, CA 91604
(818) 623-8994

Barbara Cohen, C.S.A.
(See Artz/Cohen Casting)

Chadwick Cohn
& Chadwick Struck
Thunderstruck Casting
11718 Barrington Ct., Ste. 265
Los Angeles, CA 90049
(310) 572-2898

Joanna Colbert
(See Universal Studios)

Aisha Coley
7336 Santa Monica Boulevard, #611
West Hollywood, CA 90046
(323) 882-4144

Annelise Collins Casting, C.S.A.,
C.C.D.A.
3435 Ocean Park Avenue, Ste. 112
Santa Monica, CA 90405
(310) 586-1936
Web site: www.annelisecast.com
(See also The Casting Studios)

Anya Colloff
(323) 956-4710
(See CFB Casting)

Columbia/TriStar
Domestic Television
9336 West Washington Boulevard
Culver City, CA 90232
(310) 202-3444

Craig Colvin Casting
Chelsea Studios
11530 Ventura Boulevard
Studio City, CA 91604
(818) 762-1900
5th Street Studios
1216 5th Street
Santa Monica, CA 90401
(818) 458-1100

Compassionate Casting
5th Street Studios
1216 5th Street
Santa Monica, CA 90401
(310) 458-1100

Ruth Conforte, C.S.A.
3620 Barham Boulevard,
Building Y, #201
Los Angeles, CA 90068
(818) 771-7287

M.R. Cooper Casting
2850 Potomac Avenue
Los Angeles, CA 90016
(323) 730-1164

Cara Coslow
Carsey Werner Mandabach Company
Vice President of Casting
CBS Studio Center
4024 Radford Avenue, Building 3
Studio City, CA 91604
(818) 655-6218

Dan Cowan
(323) 937-0411
(See Lien/Cowan Casting)

Allison Cowitt, C.S.A.
(818) 501-0177
(See Fenton-Cowitt Casting)

Elaine Craig Voice Casting, Inc.
C.C.D.A.
6464 Sunset Boulevard, Ste. 1150
Los Angeles, CA 90028
(323) 469-8773
Web site: www.elainecraig.com

Crash Casting-Commercials
(See On Your Mark)

Creative Extras Casting (CEC)
2461 Santa Monica Boulevard, #501
Santa Monica, CA 90404
(310) 395-8233
Registration: (310) 203-7860
Hotline: (310) 203-1459

Dianne Crittenden
2321 Abbott Kinney, #200
Venice, CA 90291
(310) 827-7730

Patrick Cunningham, C.S.A.
2630 Lacy Street
Los Angeles, CA 90031
(323) 222-1656
e-mail: pscrox@aol.com
Fax: (323) 225-7815

Joe D'Agosta
(310) 652-8123

Billy Damota
c/o Chelsea Studios
11530 Ventura Boulevard
Studio City, CA 91604
(818) 762-1900

Bill Dance Casting
4605 Lankershim Boulevard, Ste. 401
North Hollywood, CA 91602
(818) 754-6634
Registration Info: (818) 754-6633
Web site: BillDanceCasting.com

Anita Dann, C.S.A.
(See C.S.A.)

Eric Dawson, C.S.A.
(See Ulrich/Dawson/Kritzer Casting)

Shawn Dawson, C.S.A.
(See Ulrich/Dawson/Kritzer Casting)

Richard De Lancy
4741 Laurel Canyon Boulevard,
Ste. 100
North Hollywood, CA 91607
(818) 760-3110
Web site: www.delancy.com

Zora DeHorter
(310) 586-8964
Fax: (310) 586-8692
(See Weber & Associates Casting)

DeLaurentiis Productions
10061 Riverside Drive, Ste. 101
Toluca Lake, CA 91602
(909) 599-5838

Elina DeSantos
P.O. Box 1718
Santa Monica, CA 904506
(310) 829-5958

DIC Entertainment
303 North Glenoaks Boulevard, 4th Fl.
Burbank, CA 91502
(818) 955-5400

Dickson-Arbusto Casting
3875 Wilshire Boulevard, Ste. 701
Los Angeles, CA 90010
(213) 739-0556

Concetta Di Matteo
(See Long/Di Matteo Casting)

Disney Channel
3800 West Alameda Avenue, Ste. 529
Burbank, CA 91505
(818) 569-7500

Disney Feature Animation
2100 Riverside Drive
Burbank, CA 91506
(818) 460-8000

Divisek Casting, C.C.D.A.
6420 Wilshire Boulevard, Ste. LL100
Los Angeles, CA 90048
(323) 655-7766

Pam Dixon
P.O. Box 6732
Beverly Hills, CA 90213
(310) 271-8064

Warner Bros.
4000 Warner Boulevard, Building 76
Burbank, CA 91522
(818) 3918

Michael Donovan Casting, C.S.A., C.C.D.A.
8907 Wilshire Boulevard, Ste. 200
Beverly Hills, CA 90211
(310) 657-2820
Fax: (310) 657-2830
Web site:
www.conovanandhardwick.com

Christy Dooley
CBS Television
7800 Beverly Boulevard, #3371
Los Angeles, CA 90036
(323) 665-1776

Brian Dorfman
(See Touchstone Television/ABC
Entertainment Television Group)

Dowd/Reudy Casting
The Casting Studios
5724 West Third Street, #508
Los Angeles, CA 90036

Mary Downey Productions
705 North Kenwood
Burbank, CA 91505
(818) 563-1200
Fax: (818) 563-1585

DreamWorks Casting
100 Universal City Plaza,
Building 10, 27th Fl.
Universal City, CA 91608
(818) 6 95-5000

Jennifré DuMont
(323) 270-2278

Dorian Dunas, C.S.A.
(See C.S.A.)

Nan Dutton, C.S.A.
14950 Calvert Street
Van Nuys, CA 91411
(See also C.S.A.)

Carolyn Dyer
14118 Archwood Street
Van Nuys, CA 90036
(323) 954-2400

E! Entertainment Television
5750 Wilshire Boulevard
Los Angeles, CA 90036
(323) 954-2400

Abra Edelman
(See Goodman/Edelman Casting)

Susan Edelman, C.S.A.
(See Buck Edelman Casting)

Kathryn Eisenstein, C.S.A.
(See C.S.A.)
(310) 788-6712

Donna Ekholdt, C.S.A.
Big Ticket Television
Sunset-Gower Studios
1438 North Gower, Bldg. 35, Box 45
Los Angeles, CA 90028
(323) 860-7425

Judy Elkins Casting, C.C.D.A.
Chelsea Studios
11530 Ventura Boulevard
Studio City, CA 91604
(818) 762-1900

Britt Enggren
(See Rodeo Casting)

Steven Erdek
(See Westside Casting)

Danielle Eskinazi Casting, C.C.D.A.
1641 North Ivar Street
Los Angeles, CA 90028
(323) 465-9999

Felicia Fasano
(See Betty Mae Casting)

Liz Lang Fedrick
(See Mackey/Sandrich Casting)

Leslee Feldman
(See Dreamworks Casting)

Fenton-Cowitt Casting, C.S.A.
16311 Ventura Boulevard, #255
Encino, CA 91436
(818) 501-0177

Lisa Fields Casting
Silverlayne Studios
1161 North Las Palma
Los Angeles, CA 90048
(323) 468-6888

Sarah Halley Finn
See Finn/Hiller Casting

Mali Finn Casting
303 North Sweetzer Avenue
Los Angeles, CA 90048
(323) 782-8744

Finn/Hiller Casting
588 North Larchmont Boulevard
Los Angeles, CA 90004
(323) 460-4530

Moira R. Fitzmaurice
(See Katy & Co.)

Julia Flores
9121 Atlantic Avenue, #430
Huntington Beach, CA 92646
(714) 965-4669

Megan Foley Commercial Casting,
C.C.D.A.
Chelsea Studios
11530 Ventura Boulevard
Studio City, CA 91604
(818) 762-1900

FOX Broadcasting Company
10201 West Pico Boulevard
Los Angeles, CA 90035
(310) 369-1000

Farrah Fox-Collis
(See UPN)

Eddie Foy III
Dick Clark Productions
2920 West Olive Avenue, Ste. 106
Burbank, CA 91505
(818) 841-6287

Nancy Foy, C.S.A.
(See C.S.A.)

Linda Francis
8833 Sunset Boulevard, #202
West Hollywood, CA 90069
(310) 289-5974

Delia Frankel
(See Columbia Tristar TV)

Jerold Franks & Associates, C.S.A.
(323) 874-1901
(See C.S.A.)

Carrie Frazier, C.S.A.
(310) 201-9537
(See HBO)
Casts features through agents only.

Lisa Freiberger, C.S.A.
(323) 468-3215
(See C.S.A.)

Dean Fronk
(818) 325-1289
(See Pemrick/Fronk Casting)

Jean Sarah Frost, C.S.A.
(See C.S.A.)

Funky Ferrets Casting
P.O. Box 8229
Los Angeles, CA 90048
(323) 954-0007

Dennis Gallegos Casting
639 North Larchmont Boulevard,
#207
Los Angeles, CA 90004
(323) 469-3577

Nicole Garcia
c/o MADTV
Hollywood Center Studios
1048 North Las Palmas, Bldg. 3
Hollywood, CA 90038
(323) 860-8975

Risa Bramon Garcia, C.S.A.
(See C.S.A.)

Melinda Gartzman
11271 Ventura Boulevard, #248
Studio City, CA 91604
(818) 506-6962

Scott Genkinger
(See Junie Lowry-Johnson Casting)

Casting By Jeff Gerrard
c/o Big House Studios
4420 Lankershim Boulevard
North Hollywood, CA 91602
(818) 752-7100

Michelle Gertz Casting
100 Universal City Plaza
Building 2160, 8th Fl.
Universal City, CA 91608
(818) 777-7581
(See also Universal Studios Feature
Film Casting)

Dan Gibson
(323) 954-2446
(See E! Entertainment Television)

David Giella, C.S.A.
Giella/Dunlop Casting
12711 Ventura Boulevard, Ste. 280
Studio City, CA 91604
(818) 508-3361

Janet Gilmore
Raleigh Manhattan Beach Studios
1600 Rosencrans Avenue, Bldg. 4-B,
1st Fl.
Manhattan Beach, CA 90266
(310) 727-2290

Jan Glaser, C.S.A.
(See Gerald I. Wolff & Associates)

Laura Gleason Casting, C.S.A.
19528 Ventura Boulevard, #370
Tarzana, CA 91356
(818) 881-6643

Charisse Glenn Casting, C.C.D.A.
Fifth Street Studios
1216 Fifth Street
Santa Monica, CA 90401
(310) 458-1100

Susan Glicksman Casting, C.S.A.
(310) 305-2222

Vicki Goggin
Vicki Goggin & Associates Casting
Chelsea Studios
11530 Ventura Boulevard
Studio City, CA 91604
(818) 762-1900

Gail Goldberg
(818) 560-7509
(See Buena Vista Motion Picture
Group)

Peter Golden, C.S.A.
(See CBS)

Danny Goldman & Associates,
C.C.D.A.
1006 North Cole Avenue
Los Angeles, CA 90038
(323) 463-1600

Libby Goldstein
(See Junie Lowry-Johnson Casting)

Louis Goldstein & Associates
Casting/Paradox Casting
P.O. Box 691037
West Hollywood, CA 90069
(310) 552-8257
(See also On Your Mark)

Carol Goldwasser
CBS Radford
4024 Radford Avenue, Building 7
West, Room 28
Studio City, CA 91604
(818) 655-6762
Fax: (818) 769-3696

Jeff Golomb
(310) 238-0680

Marsha Goodman
(See DIC Entertainment)

Goodman-Edelman Casting, C.S.A.
c/o Hearst Entertainment
1640 South Sepulveda Boulevard,
4th Fl.
Los Angeles, CA 90025
(310) 473-1280
Fax: (310) 473-1680

Marilyn Granas, C.C.D.A.
220 South Palm Drive
Beverly Hills, CA 90212
(310) 278-3773
Fax: (310) 278-5359

Nancy Green-Keyes
4924 Balboa Boulevard, #371
Encino, CA 91316
(818) 759-4425

Jeff Greenberg & Associates
Paramount Studios
5555 Melrose Avenue, Marx Bros.
Bldg., #102
Los Angeles, CA 90038
(323) 956-4886

Harriet Greenspan, C.S.A.
(See C.S.A.)

Michael Greer Casting
(818) 906-3360

Aaron Griffith
8440 Santa Monica Boulevard, #200
Los Angeles, CA 90069
(323) 654-0033

Iris Grossman
(See TNT)

Al Guarino
2118 Wilshire Boulevard, #995
Santa Monica, CA 90403
(310) 829-6009

Sheila Guthrie, C.S.A.
Paramount Studios
5555 Melrose Avenue,
Balaban Bldg., Ste. A
Los Angeles, CA 90038
(323) 956-2701

Milt Hamerman, C.S.A.
(See C.S.A.)

Hampton Wilshire Casting
MMPR Productions
26030 Avenue Hall, Stsage 3
Valencia, CA 91355
(661) 294-1915
Fax: (661) 294-1016

Kim Hardin
(213) 694-0316

Jeff Hardwick
12439 Magnolia Boulevard, #296
Studio City, CA 91607
(818) 752-9898

Donise L. Hardy
Casting Works L.A.
1317 North San Fernando Boulevard,
#326
Burbank, CA 91504
(818) 556-6218
e-mail: CworksLA@aol.com

Stacey Harmen
(See Westside Casting)
Phaedra Harris Casting
2665 Main Street, Ste. 200
Santa Monica, CA 90405
(310) 392-7424

Susan Havins, C.C.D.A.
Chelsea Studios
11530 Ventura Boulevard
Studio City, CA 91604
(818) 762-1900

Lindsey Hayes
(See Mali Finn Casting)

René Haynes, C.S.A.
1314 Scott Road
Burbank, CA 91504
(818) 842-0187

HBO
2049 Century Park East, 36th Fl.
Los Angeles, CA 90067
(310) 201-9200

Helgoth and Associates Casting
1607 North El Centro, Ste. 19
Hollywood, CA 90028
(323) 462-5021
e-mail: Helgocast@aol.com

Henderson-Zuckerman Casting
16161 Ventura Boulevard, #106
Encino, CA 91436
(818) 788-8909

Richard Hicks Casting, C.S.A.
(See C.S.A.)

Randi Hiller
(See Finn/Hiller Casting)

Marc Hirschfeld, C.S.A.
(See NBC)

Janet Hirshenson, C.S.A.
(See The Casting Company)

**Hispanic Talent Casting
of Hollywood**
P.O. Box 46123
Los Angeles, CA 90046
(323) 934-6465

Beth Holmes Casting, C.C.D.A.
Loudmouth Studios
13261 Moorpark Street
Sherman Oaks, CA 91423
(818) 501-5625

Judith Holstra & Associates
13731 Ventura Boulevard, Ste. B
Sherman Oaks, CA 91423

Bill Hooey
(See Hispanic Talent Casting of
Hollywood)

Bob Huber
(See FOX Broadcasting Company)

Victoria Huff, C.S.A.
5700 Wilshire Boulevard,
Ste. 500 North
Los Angeles, CA 90036
(323) 634-1260

Julie Hutchinson, C.S.A.
(See 20th Century-Fox)
(310) 369-1892

Elaine Huzzar
(310) 821-7272

Hymson-Ayer Casting
5225 Wilshire Boulevard, Ste. 408
Los Angeles, CA 90036
(323) 965-5488

Idolmakers Casting
(See On Your Mark)

Donna Isaacson, C.S.A.
(See 20th Century-Fox, Bldg. 12,
Room 201)
(310) 369-1824

Rick Jacobs
Lifetime Television
Head of Talent
2049 Century Park East, Ste. 840
Los Angeles, CA 90067
(310) 556-7564

Amber Jarrett
The Casting Ste.
3518 Cahuenga Boulevard West,
Ste. 100
Los Angeles, CA 90068
(310) 582-1796

Jane Jenkins, C.S.A.
(See The Casting Company)
(323) 938-0700

Lorna Johnson
8615 Tamarack
Sun Valley, CA 91352
(818) 252-6155

Allison Jones
4063 Radford Avenue, Ste. 110
Studio City, CA 91604
(818) 754-5465

Caro Jones, C.S.A.
P.O. Box 3329
Los Angeles, CA 90078
(323) 664-0460

Kalin/Todd Casting
(See also listing under New York
Casting Directors)
(310) 284-4977

**Kalmenson & Kalmenson
Voice Casting**
5730 Wish Avenue
Encino, CA 91316 (Mailing Address)
105 South Sparks Street
Burbank, CA 91506
(Auditions/Classes)
(818) 342-6499
Fax: (818) 343-1403
e-mail: Kalmenson@earthliknk.net
Web site: www.Kalmenson.com

Alan Kaminsky
Danny Goldman & Associates
1006 North Cole Avenue
Los Angeles, CA 90038
(323) 463-1600

Ellie Kanner, C.S.A.
10880 Wilshire Boulevard, Ste. 1101
Los Angeles, CA 90024
(310) 234-5082

Christian Kaplan, C.S.A.
(See 20th Century-Fox, Bldg. 12,
Room 201)
(310) 369-1883

Tracy Kaplan, C.S.A.
(See C.S.A.)
(310) 559-3306

Kerry Karsian, C.S.A.
(See C.S.A.)

Lisa Miller Katz, C.S.A.
4000 Warner Boulevard, Building 131
Burbank, CA 91522
(818) 954-7586

Sarah Elizabeth Katzman, C.S.A.
(See C.S.A.)
(323) 468-6633

Kelly Casting
Chelsea Studios
11503 Ventura Boulevard
Studio City, CA 91604
(818) 762-1900

Lora Kennedy
(See Warner Bros. Features Casting)

Peggy Kennedy
(See Pagano/Manwiller Casting)

Lee Sonya Kissik
Magic Casting
1660 Cougar Ridge Road
Buellton, CA 93427
(805) 688-3702

Amy Klein, C.S.A.
12021 Wilshire Boulevard, #263
Los Angeles, CA 90025
(310) 478-6068

Beth Klein
(See Viacom Productions)

Heidi Klein
Klein Casting
(818) 759-6761

Robin Klein
Klein Casting
(818) 759-6761

Thom Klohn, C.S.A.
(See C.S.A.)

Cheryl Kloner
(See Liberman/Patton Casting)

Nancy Klopper, C.S.A.
(See C.S.A.)

Kathy Knowles
Fifth Avenue Studios
1216 Fifth Street
Santa Monica, CA 90401
(310) 458-1100

Joanne Koehler, C.S.A.
(See C.S.A.)

Dorothy Koster Casting, C.S.A.
Crystal Sky Productions
1901 Avenue of the Stars, Ste. 605
Los Angeles, CA 90067
(310) 843-0223

Annamarie Kostura
(See NBC)

Ronna Kress, C.S.A.
(See C.S.A.)

Carol Kritzer, C.S.A.
(See Ulrich/Dawson/Kritzer Casting)

Deborah Kurtz, C.C.D.A.
1345 Abbot Kinney Boulevard
Venice, CA 90291
(310) 452-6800

Donald Kushner
11601 Wilshire Boulevard, 21st Fl.
Los Angeles, CA 90025
(310) 445-1111

Ross Lacy Casting
The Casting Studios
5724 West 3rd Street, #508
Los Angeles, CA 90036
(310) 358-7558

Ruth Lambert, C.S.A.
(See C.S.A.)

Linda Lamontagne
Karen Vice Casting
4705 Laurel Canyon, 4th Fl.
Valley Village, CA 91607
(818) 752-5856

Landau Casting, C.C.D.A.
Fifth Street Studios
1216 5th Street
Santa Monica, CA 90401
(310) 458-1100

Shana Landsburg, C.S.A.
14852 Ventura Boulevard, Ste. 203
Sherman Oaks, CA 91403
(818) 981-4995

Meredith Layne
Big Ticket Television
Sunset-Gower Studios
1438 North Gower, Bldg. 35, Box 45
Los Angeles, CA 90028
(323) 860-7425

Sally Lear, C.S.A.
838 North Fairfax Avenue
Los Angeles, CA 90046
(323) 658-5210

Geraldine Leder, C.S.A.
(See C.S.A.)
Keli Lee, C.S.A.
(See Touchstone Television/ABC
Entertainment Television)
(818) 560-6566

Carol Lefko
P.O. Box 84509
Los Angeles, CA 90073
(310) 888-0007

Alexa Leskys
(See Viacom Productions)

Kathleen Letterie, C.S.A.
(See The WB)

John Frank Levey, C.S.A.
(See Warner Bros. TV)

Gail Levin
(See Paramount Pictures Features
Casting)

Levinson/Arnold Casting
2941 Main Street, Ste. 300 B
Santa Monica, CA 90405

Heidi Levitt Casting, C.S.A
7201 Melrose Avenue, Ste. 203
Los Angeles, CA 90046
(323) 525-0800

Liberman/Patton Casting
4311 Wilshire Boulevard, #606
Los Angeles, CA 90010
(323) 525-1381
Fax: (323) 525-0131

Amy Lieberman
(See Mark Taper Forum)

Sharon Chazin Lieblein, C.S.A.
(See Nickelodeon)

Lien/Cowan Casting, C.C.D.A.
7461 Beverly Boulevard, Ste. 203
Los Angeles, CA 90036
(323) 937-0411

Tracy Lilienfield, C.S.A.
CBS Studio Center
4024 Radford Avenue, Bungalow 1
Studio City, CA 91604
(818) 655-5652

Amy Lippens Casting
8660 Hayden Place, 2nd Fl.
Culver City, CA 90232
(310) 840-7470
Fax: (310) 840-7468

Robin Lippin, C.S.A.
846 North Cahuenga Boulevard,
Bldg. D
Hollywood, CA 90038

Marci Liroff
P.O. Box 48498
Los Angeles, CA 90048
(323) 876-3900

Leslie Litt, C.S.A.
(See Warner Bros. TV)

London-Stroud Casting
(See C.S.A.)

Beverly Long, C.C.D.A.
Moorpark Studios
11425 Moorpark Street
Studio City, CA 91602
(818) 754-6222

Carolyn Long
(See Long/Di Matteo Casting)

Long/Di Matteo Casting
The Bakery
10709 Burbank Boulevard
North Hollywood, CA 91601
(310) 225-5267

Molly Lopata, C.S.A.
13731 Ventura Boulevard, Ste. A
Sherman Oaks, CA 91423
(818) 788-0673

**Junie Lowry-Johnson
Casting,** C.S.A.
c/o 20th Century-Fox
10201 West Pico Boulevard, Bochco
Bldg., Room 232
Los Angeles, CA 90035
(323) 956-4856
c/o Paramount
5555 Melrose Avenue
Von Sternberg Bldg., Rm. 104
Los Angeles, CA 90028

Linda Lowy Casting, C.S.A.
5225 Wilshire Boulevard, Ste. 718
Los Angeles, CA 90036
(323) 634-0700

Penny Ludford Casting
100 Hurlbut Street, Unit 9
Pasadena, CA 91105
(626) 799-0919

MacDonald/Bullington Casting
1645 North Vine Street, 8th Fl.
Hollywood, CA 90028
(323) 468-0599

Betty Mae Casting
1023 1/2 Abbot Kinney Boulevard
Venice, CA 90291
(310) 396-6100

Suzie MaGrey
(See On Your Mark)

Francine Maisler, C.S.A.
Sony Pictures
10202 West Washington Boulevard
Jimmy Stewart Building, Room 207
Culver City, CA 90232
(310) 244-6945

Mambo Casting
1139 Hacienda Place
West Hollywood, CA 90069
(323) 650-9190
Fax: (323) 650-9194

Marilyn Mandel Casting
P.O. Box 691044
West Hollywood, CA 90069
(310) 271-2527

Ann Maney
(See 20th Century Fox Television)

Sheila Manning
508 South San Vicente Boulevard
Los Angeles, CA 90048
(323) 852-1046

Debi Manwiller, C.S.A.
(See Pagano/Manwiller Casting)

Karen & Mary Margiotta
8060 Melrose Avenue, Ste. 400
West Hollywood, CA 90046
(323) 658-1115

Irene Mariano, C.S.A.
(See C.S.A.)

Mindy Marin
Bluewater Ranch Entertainment Inc.
Casting Artists, Inc.
1433 6th Street
Santa Monica, CA 90401
(310) 395-1882

Martin Casting
c/o Chelsea Studios
11530 Ventura Boulevard
Studio City, CA 91604
(818) 762-1900

Tony Martinelli
(See 20th Century Fox TV)

Liz Marx, C.S.A.
(See C.S.A.)

Ricki G. Maslar
5050 Coldwater Canyon, PH 6
Sherman Oaks, CA 91423
(818) 761-8986
Fax: (818) 509-8972

Laray Mayfield
Village Studio
519 Broadway
Santa Monica 90401
(310) 656-4600

Brigid McBride
(See Westside Casting)

Hank McCann
1045 Gayley Avenue, Ste. 200
Los Angeles, CA 90024
(310) 443-9650

Barbara McCarthy
(See Paramount Pictures Features
Casting)

**Jeanne McCarthy & Juel
Bestrop Casting**
5225 Wilshire Boulevard, Ste. 418
Los Angeles, CA 90036
(323) 934-8363

Megan McConnell
Raleigh Manhattan Beach Studios
1600 Rosencrans Avenue,
Bldg. 4-B, 1st Fl.
Manhattan Beach, CA 90266
(310) 727-2290

Cydney McCurdy
2460 North Lake Avenue, Ste. 111
Altadena, CA 91001
(818) 569-3055

Kelly McDonald
(See Spelling Television, Inc.)

Robert McGee, C.S.A.
(See C.S.A.)

Vivian McRae, C.S.A.
P.O. Box 1351
Burbank, CA 91507
(818) 848-9690

McSharry-Warshaw Casting
3000 South Robertson Boulevard,
Ste. 245
Los Angeles, CA 90034
(310) 558-5047

Pat Melton
3960 Ince Boulevard, Room 103
Culver City, CA 90232
(310) 202-4992

Gina Merrill
(See E! Entertainment Television)

Jeff Meshel, C.S.A.
(See NBC)

Monika Mikkelsen
(See Heidi Levitt Casting)

Barbara Miller, C.S.A.
(See Warner Bros. TV)
(818) 954-7645

Kevin Miller Casting
c/o Chelsea Studios
11530 Ventura Boulevard
Studio City, CA 91604
(818) 762-1900
(310) 358-7021

Anna Camille Miller-Sharma
Indigo Films
5400 McConnell Avenue
Los Angeles, CA 90066
(310) 448-7182

Rick Millikan, C.S.A.
20th Century Fox
10201 West Pico Boulevard,
Building 71
Los Angeles, CA 90035
(310) 369-2772

Mionie/Stringer Casting
(See C.S.A.)

Ed Mitchell
1247 Lincoln Boulevard, Ste. 302
Santa Monica, CA 90401

Shannon Monahan Casting
7212 Pomelo Drive
West Hills, CA 91307
(818) 888-9948

Rick Montegomery Casting
(310) 841-5969

Bob Morones Casting
4130 Cahuenga Boulevard, Ste. 309
Universal City, CA 91602

Donna Morong, C.S.A.
(See Buena Vista Motion Picture
Group)
(818) 560-7875

Michelle Morris Gertz, C.S.A.
(See Michelle Gertz Casting)

Mossberg/Anthony Casting
18975 Century Park East
Los Angeles, CA 90067
(310) 444-8370

Helen Mossler, C.S.A.
(See Paramount Pictures TV Casting)
(323) 956-5578

MTV Network
2600 Colorado Avenue
Santa Monica, CA 90404

John Mulkeen Casting
(See also On Your Mark)
1728 Alvira Street
Los Angeles, CA 90035
(323) 938-6556

Roger Mussenden, C.S.A. &
Elizabeth Torres, C.S.A.
10536 Culver Boulevard, Ste. C
Culver City, CA 90232
(310) 559-9522

Brian Myers
4924 Radford Avenue, Bungalow 5
Studio City, CA 91604

Robin Nassif, C.S.A.
(See C.S.A.)

Nancy Nayor Casting, C.S.A.
6320 Commodore Sloat Drive
Los Angeles, CA 90048
(323) 857-0151

NBC
3000 West Alameda Avenue
Burbank, CA 91523
(818) 840-3774

Debra Neathery
4820 North Cleon Avenue
North Hollywood, CA 91601
(818) 506-5524

Bruce H. Newberg, C.S.A.
(See C.S.A.)
(323) 468-6633

Nickelodeon
2600 Colorado Avenue, 2nd Fl.
Santa Monica, CA 90404

Nicolau Casting, C.S.A., C.C.D.A.
8910 Holly Place
Los Angeles, CA 90046
(323) 650-9899

Sonia Nikore, C.S.A.
(See NBC)
(818) 840-3835

Patricia Noland
NBC Productions
330 Bob Hope Drive, Trailer B
Burbank, CA 91523
(818) 840-7676

Wendy O'Brien, C.S.A.
automatic sweat
221 North Robertson Boulevard, #F
Beverly Hills, CA 90211
(310) 271-2650

Pauline O'Con
(See Fox Broadcasting Company)

Michael O'Connel
(See MacDonald/Bullington Casting)

Jenny O'Haver & Company
C.C.D.A.
(323) 650-9010
(See also On Your Mark)

Meryl O'Loughlin, C.S.A.
(See C.S.A.)

On Location Casting
1223 Wilshire Boulevard, PMB #409
Santa Monica, CA 90403
(310) 772-8181
Talent Hotline: (310) 284-3549

On Your Mark
451 North La Cienega Boulevard, #12
Los Angeles, CA 90048
(310) 360-9936

Lori Openden, C.S.A.
(See C.S.A.)

Kim Orchen
(See Disney Channel)

Fern Orenstein, C.S.A.
(See CBS)

Gregory Orson
9171 Wilshire Boulevard, Ste. 400
Beverly Hills, CA 91210
(310) 205-6906

Raquel Osborne
235 East Colorado Boulevard, #189
Pasadena, CA 91101

Jessica Overwise, C.S.A.
17250 Sunset Boulevard, #304
Pacific Palisades, CA 90272
(310) 459-2686

Pagano-Manwiller Casting, C.S.A.
3815 Hughes Avenue, 4th Fl.
Culver City, CA 90232
(310) 841-4320
e-mail: Pagano-Manwiller@onebox.com

Marvin Paige, C.S.A.
P.O. Box 69964
West Hollywood, CA 90069
(818) 760-3040

Sam Pancake
(See Dowd/Reudy Casting)

Pantone Casting, C.C.D.A.
1662 Hillhurst Avenue
Los Angeles, C A 90027

John Papsidera, C.S.A.
automatic sweat
221 North Robertson Boulevard, Ste. F
Beverly Hills, CA 90211

**Paramount Pictures
Features Casting**
Paramount Studios
5555 Melrose Avenue,
Bob Hope Building,
Room 206
Hollywood, CA 90038
(323) 956-5444
Fax: (323) 862-1371

**Paramount Pictures
Television Casting**
Paramount Studios
5555 Melrose Avenue, Bluhdorn Bldg.,
Room 128
Hollywood, CA 90038
(323) 956-5578

Jennifer Fishman Pate
(See CFB Casting)

Cami Patton, C.S.A.
(See Liberman/Patton Casting)

Joey Paul
Sunset Gower Studios
1438 North Gower, Box 13
Hollywood, CA 90028

Pemrick/Fronk Casting
14724 Ventura Boulevard, Penthouse
Sherman Oaks, CA 91403
(818) 325-1289

Nancy Perkins
(See Universal Studios Television)

Penny Perry
P.O. Box 57677
Sherman Oaks, CA 91413
(310) 315-4868

Kari Peyton Casting
1145 North McCadden Place
Los Angeles, CA 90038
(323) 462-1500
Fax: (323) 462-1661

Jack Phelan
6919 Valjean Avenue
Van Nuys, CA 91406

Bonnie Pietila
20th Century Fox
10201 West Pico Boulevard,
Trailer 730
Los Angeles, CA 90035
(310) 369-3632

Gayle Pillsbury
(See Zane Pillsbury Casting)

Plaster Casting
1161 North Las Palmas Boulevard
Los Angeles, CA 90038

Christy Pokarney
Omega Entertainment
8760 Shoreham Drive
Los Angeles, CA 90069
(310) 855-0516

Holly Powell, C.S.A.
5542 Satsuma Drive
North Hollywood, CA 91601

Lynne Quirion
Chelsea Studios
11530 Ventura Boulevard
Studio City, CA 91604
(818) 762-1900

Pamela Rack, C.S.A.
(See C.S.A.)

Claudia Ramsumair
(See The WB)

Mark Randall Casting
1811 North Whitley, #401
Los Angeles, CA 90028
(323) 465-7553

Johanna Ray & Associates, C.S.A.
1022 Palm Avenue, #2
West Hollywood, CA 90069
(310) 652-2511)

Robyn Ray, C.S.A.
(See C.S.A.)

Robi Reed & Associates
6605 Hollywood Boulevard, Ste. 100
Los Angeles, CA 90028

Joe Reich
Supervisor, Casting Administration
Walt Disney Television
2600 West Olive Avenue, #1034
Burbank, CA 91506
(818) 955-6813

**Barbara Remsen
& Associates,** C.S.A.
Raleigh Studios
650 North Bronson Avenue, Ste. 124
Los Angeles, CA 90004
(323) 464-7968

Joan Renfrow
Onyx Productions
5550 Wilshire Boulevard, Ste. 301
Los Angeles, CA 90036
(323) 692-9830

Gretchen Rennell-Court, C.S.A.
(See C.S.A.)

Tom Reudy
(323) 954-0007
(See Dowd/Reudy Casting)

Phyllis Ricci
(See On Your Mark)

Rodeo Casting
7013 Willoughby Avenue
Los Angeles, CA 90038
(323) 969-9125

Romano/Benner Casting
800 South Main Street, Ste. 222
Burbank, CA 91506

Stacey Rosen, C.S.A.
(See C.S.A.)

Paula Rosenberg, C.S.A.
818 12th Street, Ste. 9
Santa Monica, Ca 90403
(310) 260-0129
e-mail: Grace_12929@aol.com

Vicki Rosenberg & Associates
10201 West Pico Boulevard, #80/10
Los Angeles, CA 90035
(310) 369-3448

Donna Rosenstein
c/o Disney
500 SouthBuena Vista Street
Burbank, CA 91521
(818) 560-7837

Eleanor Ross, C.S.A.
(See C.S.A.)

Marcia Ross, C.S.A.
(See Buena Vista Motion Picture
Group)
(818) 560-7510

Renée Rousselot, C.S.A.
(See C.S.A.)

Orlette Ruiz
(See Mambo Casting)

Patrick Rush Casting, C.S.A.
10202 West Washington Boulevard
Jimmy Stewart Bldg., Room 26
Culver City, CA 90232
(310) 244-7973

Saban Entertainment
10960 Wilshire Boulevard, 3rd Fl.
Los Angeles, CA 90024
(310) 235-5102

Marnie Saitta
"The Young and the Restless"
CBS
7800 Beverly Boulevard, Ste. 3305
Los Angeles, CA 90036
(323) 575-2803

Tess Sanchez
(See The WB)

Michael Sanford
(See On Your Mark)

Gabrielle Scharry, C.C.D.A.
Sessions West Studios
2601 Ocean Park Boulevard, Ste. 201
Santa Monica, CA 90405
(310) 450-0835

Laura Schiff
1600 Rosencrans Avenue
Building 4B, 1st Fl.
Manhattan Beach, CA 90266
(310) 727-2955

Arlene Schuster-Goss, C.C.D.A.
(See ASG Casting)

Emily Schweber
1024 North Palm Avenue
West Hollywood, CA 90069
(310) 360-1144

Jean Scoccimarro, C.S.A.
(See C.S.A.)

Brien Scott, C.S.A.
18034 Ventura Boulevard, Ste. 2175
Encino, CA 91316
(818) 343-3669

Kevin Scott, C.S.A.
(818) 954-5138
(See Warner Bros. TV)

Tina Seiler
P.O. Box 46321
Los Angeles, CA 90046
(818) 382-7929

Lila Selik Casting, C.C.D.A.
1551 South Robertson Boulevard,
#202
Los Angeles, CA 90035
(310) 556-2444
Web site:
www.pozproductions.com/selik.htm

Francene Selkirk, C.C.D.A.
Shooting From The Hip Casting
Zydeco Studios
11317 Ventura Boulevard
Studio City, CA 91604
(818) 506-0613

Selzer/Freeman Casting, C.S.A.
(See C.S.A.)

Tony Sepulveda, C.S.A.
(818) 954-7639
(See Warner Bros. Television)

Sessions West Studios
2601 Ocean Park Boulevard, Ste. 201
Santa Monica, CA 90405
(310) 450-0835

Pamela Shae
(See Spelling Television Inc.)

Shaner/Testa Casting, C.S.A.
3875 Wilshire Boulevard, Ste. 700
Los Angeles, CA 90010
(213) 382-3375

Barbara Shannon
(619) 24-9555

Christine Sheaks, C.S.A.
(See C.S.A.)

Bill Shepard, C.S.A.
(See C.S.A.)

Ava Shevitt
Village Studio
519 Broadway
Santa Monica, CA 90401
(310) 656-5600

Showtime Network
(See Viacom)

Jennifer Shull, C.S.A.
(See C.S.A.)

Marcia Shulman
(See Fox Broadcasting Company)

Mark Sikes, C.S.A.
Pioneer Valley Productions
8909 Olympic Boulevard, #120
Los Angeles, CA 90211
(310) 652-9599

Margery Simkin, C.S.A.
(See C.S.A.)

Joan Simmons
4841 First Avenue
Seal Beach, CA 90740
(310) 430-7392
e-mail: JRS-Presents@Prodigy.Net

Clair Sinnett Casting
945 Sheldon Street
El Segundo, CA 90045
(310) 606-0813
Fax: (310) 606-0823
e-mail: sinnett@earthliknk.net

Melissa Skoff Casting, C.S.A.
c/o Sunset/Gower Studios
1438 North Gower Street
Bldg. #21, 1st Fl. Casting
Hollywood, CA 90028
(323) 468-4556
Fax: (323) 468-4555

Slater/Brooksbank Casting
c/o Sony Pictures Studios
10202 West Washington Boulevard
Jimmy Stewart Bldg., Ste. 26E
Culver City, CA 90232

Tammy Smith
520 Washington, Ste. 401
Marina Del Ray, CA 90292
(310) 364-3521

J.S. Snyder & Associates
1801 North Kingsley Drive, #202
Los Angeles, CA 90027
(323) 465-4241

Stephen Snyder
(See J.S. Snyder & Associates)
(323) 465-4241

Sharon Soble, C.S.A.
(See C.S.A.)

Sobo Casting
Castaway Studios
8899 Beverly Boulevard, Lobby
Los Angeles, CA 90048
(310) 248-5296

Christi Soper
(See DreamWorks Casting)
(818) 733-9854

Spelling Television
5700 Wilshire Boulevard, Ste. 575
Los Angeles, CA 90036
(323) 965-5784

Pamela Starks Casting
(323) 571-1800

Sally Stiner Casting, C.S.A.
12288 Venice Boulevard, #503
Los Angeles, CA 90066
(310) 505-6655

Stanzi Stokes Casting
(818) 762-8448

Andrea Stone, C.S.A.
(See C.S.A.)

Stuart Stone, C.C.D.A.
c/o Castaway Studios
8899 Beverly Boulevard, 1st Fl.
Los Angeles, CA 90048
(310) 248-5296
(323) 866-1811

Gilda Stratton Casting
CBS
4024 Radford Avenue,
Building 8, 2nd Fl.
Studio City, CA 91604
(818) 655-6564 CSA,
606 North Larchmont Boulevard, #4B
Los Angeles, CA 90004
(323) 463-1925

Catherine Stroud, C.S.A.
(See London/Stroud Casting)

Merri Sugarman
(See Touchstone Television/ABC
Entertainment Television Group

Ron Suma
(See June Lowry-Johnson Casting)

Monica Swann Casting, C.S.A.
12031 Ventura Boulevard, #4
Studio City, CA 91604
(818) 769-8564

Maryclaine Sweeters, C.C.D.A.
(See Westside Casting)

Yumi Takada Casting, C.C.D.A.
1830 The Strand, #3
Hermosa Beach, CA 90254
(310) 372-7287

Mark Taper Forum
601 West Temple Street
Los Angeles, CA 90012
(213) 972-7374

James F. Tarzia
Tarzia/Stockton Casting
7130 Hollywood Boulevard, Ste. 24
Hollywood, CA 90046
(323) 874-9217

Helen Taylor Casting
221 South Doheny Drive, PH B
Beverly Hills, CA 90211

Judy Taylor, C.S.A.
(See C.S.A.)

Angela Terry
(See Liberman/Patton Casting)

Mark Teschner Casting, C.S.A.
ABC Television
4151 Prospect Avenue
General Hospital Building
Los Angeles, CA 90027
(310) 557-5542

Michael Testa
(See Shaner/Testa Casting)

Jamie Thomason
Disney TV Animation
500 South Buena Vista Street
FGW Bldg., Ste. 1110
Burbank, CA 91521

Joel Thurm, C.S.A.
Hollywood Center Studios
1040 North Las Palmas, Bldg. 24
Los Angeles, CA 90038

Tillman/Johnson-Plate Casting
727 West 7th Street, #333
Los Angeles, CA 90017

TLC/Booth, Inc.
6521 Homewood Avenue
Los Angeles, CA 90028
(313) 464-2788

TNT (Turner Network Television)
1888 Century Park East, 14th Fl.
Los Angeles, CA 90067
(310) 551-6352

Joy Todd Casting Corp., C.S.A.
(See C.S.A.)
Web site: www.Joytodd.com

Tondino-Warren Casting
401 Riverside Drive
Burbank, CA 91506
(818) 843-1902

Touchstone Television/ABC
Entertainment Television Group
500 South Buena Vista Street
Burbank, CA 91521-4651
(818) 460-7313
Fax: (818) 460-6903

20th Century Fox Feature Casting
10201 West Pico Boulevard
Los Angeles, CA 90035
(310) 369-1000

20th Century Fox
Television Casting
P.O. Box 900
Beverly Hills, CA 90213-0900
(310) 369-4265

Susan Tyler Casting, C.C.D.A.
c/o Chelsea Studios
11530 Ventura Boulevard
Studio City, CA 91604
(818) 506-0400

Ulrich/Dawson/Kritzer Casting
3151 Chahuenga Boulevard West,
Ste. 345
Los Angeles, CA 90068
(323) 845-1100

Universal Studios
Feature Film Casting
100 Universal City Plaza
Bldg. 2160, Ste. 8A
Universal City, CA 91608
(818) 777-1000

Universal Studios Television
8800 Sunset Boulevard, Ste. 502
Los Angeles, CA 90069
(310) 360-2540

UPN (United Paramount Network)
11800 Wilshire Boulevard
Los Angeles, CA 90025
(310) 575-7000

Blanca Valdez
Valdez Casting En Espanol,
C.C.D.A.
1001 North Poinsettia Place
West Hollywood, CA 90046
(323) 876-5700

Nikki Valko
20th Century Fox
10201 West Pico Boulevard, Bldg.
214, Room 1
Los Angeles, CA 90035
(310) 369-2384

Raleigh Manhattan Beach Studios
1600 Rosencrans, #4B
Manhattan Beach, CA 90266

Mina Vasquez
8306 Wilshire Boulevard, #1918
Beverly Hills, CA 90211
(323) 669-1723

Paul Ventura
Chelsea Studios
11530 Ventura Boulevard
Studio City, CA 91604
(818) 762-1900

VH1
2600 Colorado Avenue
Santa Monica, CA 90404
(310) 752-8345
e-mail: Stacy.Alexander@Vh1staff.com

Viacom Productions
10880 Wilshire Boulevard, Ste. 1101
Los Angeles, CA 90024
(310) 234-5035

Karen Vice
Karen Vice Casting
4705 Laurel Canyon, 4th Fl.
Valley Village, CA 91607
(818) 752-5856

Debe Waisman Casting
11664 National Boulevard PMB #368
Los Angeles, CA 90064
(310) 558-39126
Fax: (310) 558-3920
Extra Registration Hotline:
(310) 535-1325

Dave Waite Casting
CBS Studio Center
4024 Radford Avenue, Big Trailer
Studio City, CA 91604
(818) 655-5050

Katy Wallin Casting
1918 West Magnolia Boulevard, #206
Burbank, CA 91506
(818) 563-4121

Warner Bros.
Feature Film Casting
4000 Warner Boulevard
Burbank, CA 91522
(818) 954-6000

Warner Bros. Television Casting
300 Television Plaza, Bldg. 140, 1st Fl.
Burbank, CA 91505
(818) 954-7646

Samuel Warren, C.S.A.
(See C.S.A.)
(323) 462-1510

Ted Warren
(See Tondino/Warren Casting)
(818) 843-1902

Brad Warshaw
(310) 558-5047
(See McSharry/Warshaw Casting)

The WB
411 North Hollywood Way
Building 34-R, Room 161
Burbank, CA 91505
(818) 977-6016

Mimi Webb-Miller Casting
171 Pier Avenue
Santa Monica, CA 90405
(310) 452-0863

Weber & Associates Casting
MGM
2400 Broadway Avenue, Ste. 340
Santa Monica, CA 90404
Weber Phone: (310) 449-3685
DeHorter Phone: (310) 586-8964
DeHorter Fax: (310) 586-8692

April Webster Casting
4111 West Alameda Avenue, Ste. 507
Burbank, CA 91505
(818) 556-4200

Judith Weiner
(See UPN)
(310) 575-7008

Alyssa Weisberg Casting
(310) 889-9557

Rosemary Welden, C.S.A.
(See C.S.A.)

Mary West
(See Brown/West Casting)

Westside Casting
2050 South Bundy Drive
West Los Angeles, CA 90025
(310) 820-9200

Geri Windsor, C.S.A.
(See C.S.A.)

Stacy Wise
(See Liberman/Patton Casting)

Gerald I. Wolff & Associates, Inc.
1135 South Beverly Drive, 2nd Fl.
Los Angeles, CA 90035
(310) 277-6200

Jason Wood
VP of Talent and Casting
Mandalay
1040 North Las Palmas,
Bldg. 33, Room 311
Los Angeles, CA 90038
(323) 860-3179

Gerrie Wormser Casting
2160 Century Park East
Los Angeles, CA 90067
(310) 277-3281

Douglas Wright Casting
2920 West Olive Avenue, Ste. 110
Burbank, CA 91505
(818) 556-3807

Grace Wu
(See NBC)
(818) 840-2045

Naomi Yoelin
(310) 829-9764

Rhonda Young, C.S.A.
(See C.S.A.)

Lisa Ystrom
(See Liberman/Patton Casting)

Bonnie Zane
(See Zane-Pillsbury Casting)

Debra Zane, C.S.A.
5225 Wilshire Boulevard, Ste. 601
Los Angeles, CA 90036
(323) 965-0800

Zane-Pillsbury Casting
5724 West 3rd Street, Ste. 508
Los Angeles, CA 90036
(323) 857-7230

Gary M. Zuckerbrod, C.S.A.
(818) 526-4332

Dori Zuckerman, C.S.A.
(See Henderson/Zuckerman Casting)

CHICAGO

Jane Alderman Casting
c/o Act One Studios
640 North LaSalle, Ste. 535
Chicago, IL 60610
Attn: Jane Alderman –
Casting Director
(312) 397-1182

All City Casting
P.O. Box 577640
Chicago, IL 60657-7640
Attn: June Pyskacek
(773) 588-6062

Chicago Casting Center
777 North Green Street
Chicago, IL 60622
Attn: Janet Louer, Tina O'Brien,
Siobhan Sullivan
(312) 327-1904

Esarah Casting
700 Greene Street
Chicago, IL 60622
Attn: Elizabeth Hill, Jacqueline Conard
(312) 455-8383

HollyRik & Heitz Casting
8120 44th Street
Lyons, IL 60534
Attn: Rik Kristinat or Hal Watkins
(321) 664-0601

JAZ Casting
3617 North Kedvale
Chicago, IL 60641
Attn: Jennifer Rudnicke, Cathy Kulnig
(321) 343-8111

K.T.'s
P.O. Box 577039
Chicago, IL 60657-7039
(773) 525-1126

David O'Connor Casting
1017 West Washington Street, Ste. 2A
Chicago, IL 60607
Attn: David O'Connor
(321) 226-9112

Reginacast
P.O. Box 585
Willow Springs, IL 60480
(312) 409-5521 Talent Hotline

Segal Studio
1040 West Huron Street,
Chicago, IL 60622
Attn: Jeffery Lyle Segal
(312) 563-9368

Simon Casting
1512 North Fremont Street, #202
Chicago, IL 60622
Attn: Claire Simon
(312) 202-0124

Tenner, Paskal Casting
20 West Hubbard Street, #2E
Chicago, Il 60610
Rachel Tenner, Casting Director
Mickie Paskal, Casting Director
(312) 527-0665

Trapdoor Casting
1655 West Cortland Street,
Chicago, IL 60622
Attn: Beata Pilch & Nicole Wiesner
www.trapdoortheater.com
(773) 384-0494

Umiaut Casting 4
612 North Taylor Avenue
Oak Park, IL 60302
Attn: Peter Oestreich
(312) 343-0111

Advertising Agencies Involved in Radio and TV Commercials

The following list is included because some ad agencies have their own casting directors; they are in-house and may be contacted directly.

NEW YORK AGENCIES

A Team LLC
One West 34th Street, Ste. 501
New York, NY 10001
(212) 239-0499

Abernathy MacGregor Group, Inc.
501 Madison Avenue, 13th Flr.
New York, NY 10022
(212) 371-5999

The Ad Store Inc.
33 East 30th Street
New York, NY 10016
(212) 685-8899

Adasia Communications, Inc.
137 Fifth Avenue, 5th Flr.
New York, NY 10010
(212) 358-1249

Admerasia, Inc. .
150 Lafayette Street, 5th Flr.
New York, NY 10013
(212) 686-3333

Adteam Incorporated
420 Lexington Avenue, Ste. 300
New York, NY 10170
(212) 297-6208

Advertising to Women, Inc.
36 Sutton Place
New York, NY 10022
(212) 750-4500

AdvertisingPartner.com
27 West 24th Street, Ste. 630
New York, NY 10010
(212) 337-3284

Agency.com Ltd.
20 Exchange Place
New York, NY 10005
(212) 358-2600

AKA Advertising, Inc.
215 Park Avenue South
New York, NY 10003
(212) 944-1990

Alan/Anthony Inc.
55 Broad Street, 14th Flr.
New York, NY 10004
(212) 825-1582

Albrecht Advertising & Design
230 West 17th Street
New York, NY 10011
(212) 255-6767

Allscope Media
400 Lafayette Street, 4th Flr.
New York, NY 10003
(212) 253-1300

Gavin Anderson & Co., Inc.
220 East 42nd Street, 4th Flr.
New York, NY 10017
(212) 515-1900

Authentic Marketing
40 Waterside Plaza, C203
New York, NY 10010
(212) 779-4636

Avrett, Free & Ginsburg
800 Third Avenue
New York, NY 10022
(212) 418-7331

Baldi, Bloom & Whelan Advertising
373 Park Avenue South, 8th Flr.
New York, NY 10016
(212) 679-1400

Bartle Bogle Hegarty
7 West 22nd Street, 9th Flr.
New York, NY 10010
(212) 812-6600

Bates USA (Bates Advertising USA, Inc.)
498 Seventh Avenue
New York, NY 10018
(212) 297-7000

BBDO Worldwide, Inc.
1285 Avenue of the Americas
New York, NY 10019-6095
(212) 459-5000

Bennett Book Advertising, Inc.
60 East 42nd Street, Ste. 463
New York, NY 10165
(212) 292-2990

Berenter Greehouse & Webster, Inc.
28 West 23rd Street
New York, NY 10010
(212) 727-5600

Bergman-Unger Associates
139 Perry Street
New York, NY 10014
(212) 645-1911

Berlin Cameron & Partners
1370 Broadway, 7th Flr.
New York, NY 10018
(212) 824-2000

Bezos/Nathanson Marketing Group
250 Lafayette Street
New York, NY 10012
(212) 219-3690

Bienestar LCG Communications, Inc.
230 West 41st Street, 17th Flr.
New York, NY
(212) 730-7230

Damian Bisch & Partners, Inc. Advertising
725 Fifth Avenue, 17th Flr.
New York, NY 10022
(212) 308-8855

Blu Orbit International, Inc.
920 Broadway, 3rd Flr.
New York, NY 10010
(212) 254-2663

Blue Dingo/GB
665 Broadway, 6th Flr.
New York, NY 10012-2300
(212) 358-8200

Blum Elenson Creative Network
37 West 28th Street, 7th Flr. ·
New York, NY 10001
(212) 889-0005

Booke & Company Inc.
355 Lexington Avenue, 3rd Flr.
New York, NY 10017
(212) 490-9095

Bozell Group
40 West 23rd Street
New York, NY 10010
(212) 727-5000

Brakstier & Company Inc.
419 Park Avenue South
New York, NY 10016
(212) 679-2233

The Bravo Group
230 Park Avenue South, 9th Flr.
New York, NY 10003
(212) 614-6000

Howard Bronson & Associates
6 East 45th Street, Ste. 1000
New York, NY 10017
(212) 867-6160

Brouillard Communications, Inc.
420 Lexington Avenue
New York, NY 10170
(212) 867-8300

Burkhardt & Hillman Ltd.
145 East 57th Street, 11th Flr.
New York, NY 10022
(212) 754-6060

Burson-Marsteller
230 Park Avenue South
New York, NY 10003-1566
(212) 614-4000

Lawrence Butner Advertising, Inc.
228 East 45th Street
New York, NY 10017
(212) 338-5000

Cadwell Davis Advertising
375 Hudson Street
New York, NY 10014
(212) 463-0111

Castelli Advertising
120 East 34th Street
New York, NY 10016
(212) 213-4117

CCM
470 Park Avenue South
New York, NY 10016
(212) 689-8225

Charron, Schwartz & Partners, Inc.
122 East 42nd Street, 31st Flr.
New York, NY 10168
(212) 687-5555

Charter Direct
575 Lexington Avenue, 34th Flr.
New York, NY 10022
(212) 644-0233

Chillingsworth/Radding, Inc.
35 East 21st Street, 6th Flr.
New York, NY 10010
(212) 674-4700

CiA USA, Inc.
307 East 53rd Street
New York, NY 10022
(212) 753-5200

CMG Communications, LLC
79 Fifth Avenue, 9th Flr.
New York, NY 10003
(212) 462-8200

Christy MacDougal Mitchell Inc.
Penthouse Terrace
304 East 45th Street
New York, NY 10017
(212) 661-2221

Ciociola & Company
Advertising, Inc.
30 Irving Place, 3rd Flr.
New York, NY 10003
(212) 505-6300

Circus Magazine
6 West 18th Street, 2nd Flr.
New York, NY 10011
(212) 242-4902

Citigate/Albert-Frank
850 Third Avenue, 11th Flr.
New York, NY 10022
(212) 508-3400

Clarke/Thompson
Advertising & Design
30 West 22nd Street
New York, NY 10010
(212) 645-8990

Cline, Davis & Mann, Inc.
450 Lexington Avenue
New York, NY 10017
(212) 907-4300

Communications Plus, Inc.
102 Madison Avenue
New York, NY 10016-7417
(212) 686-9570

Conill Advertising, Inc.
375 Hudson Street, 11th Flr.
New York, NY 10014
(212) 463-2500

Brian Cronin & Associates
(BCA) Inc. Advertising
370 Lexington Avenue
New York, NY 10017
(212) 286-9300

Creston & Associates, Ltd.
305 Madison Avenue, Ste. 449
New York, NY 10165
(212) 253-7264

D'Arcy Masius Benton & Bowles
1675 Broadway
New York, NY 10019
(212) 468-3622

**DDB Worldwide
Communications Group**
437 Madison Avenue
New York, NY 10022
(212) 415-2000

**Della Famina Rothschild
Jeary & Partners**
220 East 42nd Street, Ste. 500
New York, NY 10017
(212) 506-0700

Denhard & Stewart, Inc.
240 Madison Avenue
New York, NY 10016
(212) 481-3200

Deutsch, Inc.
111 Eighth Avenue
New York, NY 10011
(212) 981-7600

Dimassimo Brand Advertising
20 Cooper Square, 6th Flr.
New York, NY 10003
(212) 253-7500

DJD/Golden Advertising, Inc.
151 West 19th Street
New York, NY 10011
(212) 243-5044

E & M Advertising
462 Seventh Avenue
New York, NY 10018
(212) 981-5900

The Edelman Group
420 Lexington Avenue
New York, NY 10170
(212) 768-0550

**Elektra Entertainment Group
Advertising**
75 Rockefeller Plaza
New York, NY 10019
(212) 275-4273

Elizabeth Arden Company
200 Park Avenue South, 7th Flr.
New York, NY 10003
(212) 261-1000

Elser & Aucone, Inc.
420 Lexington Avenue, Ste. 2001
New York, NY 10170
(212) 867-3300

**Ericksen Advertising
& Design, Inc.**
12 West 37th Street
New York, NY 10018
(212) 239-3313

Exposed Brick
591 Broadway, Ste. 3A
New York, NY 10012
(212) 226-0060

**Ferrellcalvillo
Communications, Inc.**
250 Park Avenue South
New York, NY 10003
(212) 777-7077

Greco Ethridge Group
126 Fifth Avenue
New York, NY 10011
(212) 633-8973

Grey Worldwide New York
777 Third Avenue
New York, NY 10017
(212) 546-2000

**Haft Byrne Raboy
& Partners, Inc.**
111 Fifth Avenue, 10th Flr.
New York, NY 10003
(212) 674-3100

Harte-Hanks Direct
260 Madison Avenue, 20th Flr.
New York, NY 10016
(212) 889-5000

Hill & Knowlton, Inc.
466 Lexington, 8th Flr.
New York, NY 10017
(212) 885-0300

Hill-Holliday/New York
345 Hudson Street, 12th Flr.
New York, NY 10014
(212) 830-7600

Horizon Media, Inc.
630 Third Avenue
New York, NY 10017
(212) 916-8600

H2O Advertising
80 Fifth Avenue, Ste. 1108
New York, NY 10011
(212) 206-8195

Follis Advertising, Inc.
295 Park Avenue South, #PHP
New York, NY 10010
(212) 529-2461

Furman Roth Advertising
801 Second Avenue
New York, NY 10017
(212) 687-2300

G&B/Miller Advertising
71 Fifth Avenue
New York, NY 10003
(212) 366-0925

GCI Group, Inc.
777 Third Avenue, 38th Flr.
New York, NY 10017
(212) 537-8000

Gerngross & Co., Inc.
200 Varick Street
New York, NY 10014
(212) 229-0280

Gigante Vaz Partners Advertising, Inc.
The Puck Building
295 Lafayette Street, 7th Flr.
New York, NY 10012
(212) 343-0004

Gotham Advertising
550 Madison Avenue, 9th Flr.
New York, NY 10022-3211
(212) 833-4494

GRW Advertising
28 West 25th Street
New York, NY 10010
(212) 620-0549

Hunter Public Relations
41 Madison Avenue
New York, NY 10010-2202
(212) 679-6600

Independent Media Services, Inc.
880 Third Avenue, 4th Flr.
New York, NY 10022
(212) 836-8900

Initiative Media
1114 Avenue of the Americas
New York, NY 10020
(212) 218-1711

JDG Productions, Inc.
164 West 79th Street #10D
New York, NY 10024
(212) 787-9553

Jordan McGrath Case & Partners
110 Fifth Avenue
New York, NY 10011
(212) 463-1000

Katz Dochtermann & Epstein, Inc.
245 Fifth Avenue, 23rd Flr.
New York, NY 10016

Kidvertisers
270 Lafayette Street
New York, NY 10012
(212) 966-2345

KSL Media, Inc.
28 West 23rd Street
New York, NY 10010
(212) 981-5900

Leibler-Bronfman Lubalin
55 Fifth Avenue
New York, NY 10003
(212) 463-9292

Lipman, Richmond, Greene
470 Park Avenue South
New York, nY 10016
(212) 684-1100

Little & King Co., Inc.
1040 Avenue of the Americas
New York, NY 10018
(212) 278-0713

Long Advertising, Inc.
561 Broadway, 10th Flr.
New York, NY 10021
(212) 431-0600

M&C Saatchi
895 Broadway
New York, NY 10003
(212) 655-8000

Mad Dogs & Englishmen
126 Fifth Avenue, 12th Flr.
New York, NY 10011
(212) 675-6116

Manhattan Marketing Ensemble
443 Park Avenue South, 4th Flr.
New York, NY 10016
(212) 772-2233

Margeotes/Fertitta
& Partners LLC
411 Lafaeyette Street
New York, NY 10003
(212) 979-6600

Marinelli Communications, Inc.
25 East 21st Street
New York, NY 10010
(212) 254-3366

McCafftrey Rattner Gottlieb & Lane
370 Lexington Avenue
New York, NY 10017
(212) 706-8400

McCann-Erickson World Group
750 Third Avenue
New York, NY 10017
(212) 697-6000

Media Planning
1180 Avenue of the Americas 10th Flr.
New York, NY 10036
(212) 790-4800

Media Specialists, Inc.
20 East 74th Street 15A
New York, NY 10021
(212) 861-9434

Mediacom
777 Third Avenue
New York, NY 10017
(212) 546-2100

Mediavest Worldwide
1675 Broadway
New York, NY 10019
(212) 468-4000

Meier Advertising, Inc.
907 Broadway, 4th fl.
New York, NY 10010
(212) 460-5655

Merkley Newman Harty Healthworks
200 Varick Street
New York, NY 10014
(212) 366-3500

Merritt-Clapp Advertising
380 Lexington Avenue
New York, NY 10168
(212) 867-0600

Messner Vetere Berger McNamee
Schmetterer/Euro RSCG
350 Hudson Street
New York, NY 10014
(212) 886-4100

Mezzina Brown & Partners LLC
401 Park Avenue South
New York, NY 10016
(212) 251-7700

Milky Way Productions Inc.
43 West 24th Street, 6th fl.
New York, NY 10010
(212) 989-8001

Miller Advertising Agency, Inc.
71 Fifth Avenue
New York, NY 10003
(212) 929-2200

Mitchell Advertising, Inc.
39 East 30th Street, 4th fl.
New York, NY 10016
(212) 679-9359

Moss/Dragoti
437 Madison Avenue, 20th fl.
New York, NY 10022
(212) 817-6500

Nexgen Media Worldwide
157 West 57th Street
New York, NY 10019
(212) 957-7660

Norman, Lawrence, Patterson & Farrell, Inc.
358 Fifth Avenue, Penthouse
New York, NY 10001
(212) 695-8120

Ogilvy & Mather Worldwide
Head Office
309 West 49th Street
New York, NY 10019
(212) 237-4000

Omnicom Group Inc.
437 Madison Avenue, 9th fl.
New York, NY 10022
(212) 415-3600

Optimedia International
Four Herald Square
950 6th Avenue
New York, NY 10001
(212) 561-6400

Oven Digital
10 Crosby Street
New York, NY 10013-3103
(212) 253-2100

Pace Advertising
485 Fifth Avenue
New York, NY 10017
(212) 818-0100

Partners & Levit Inc.
8 West 38th Street
New York, NY 10019
(212) 696-1200

Pavlinka Chinnici Direct, LLC
411 Lafayette Street, 3rd fl.
New York, NY 10003
(212) 561-6000

Pedone & Partners
Advertising, Inc.
100 Fifth Avenue, 4th fl.
New York, NY 10011
(212) 627-3300

PK Network Communications
11 East 47th Street, 4th fl.
New York, NY 10017
(212) 888-4700

Planned Television Arts
1110 Second Avenue, 3rd fl.
New York, NY 10022
(212) 593-5820

Porter Novelli International
220 East 42nd Street
New York, NY 10017
(212) 601-8000

Powell Advertising, Inc.
233 East 32nd Street #6B
New York, NY 10016
(212) 889-7724

Rapp Collins Worldwide
11 Madison Avenue, 12th fl.
New York, NY 10010
(212) 590-7400

Rare Medium, Inc.
44 West 18th Street, Ste. 600
New York, NY 10011
(212) 634-6951

Renegade Marketing Group
75 Ninth Avenue, 4th fl.
New York, NY 10011
(646) 486-7700

RF Design
301 East 57th Street
New York, NY 10022
(212) 334-3838

Richartz Fliss Clark & Pope
317 Madison Avenue, Ste. 1522
New York, NY 10017
(212) 627-8180

RLM Public Relations Inc.
9896 6th Avenue, 14th fl.
New York, NY 10018
(212) 741-5106

Rodriguezmejer Advertising Inc.
22 East 21st Street, 7th fl.
New York, NY 10010
(212) 614-1280

Roher Public Relations
228 East 45th Street, 12th fl.
New York, NY 10017-3364
(212) 986-6668

Rubenstein Associates, Inc.
1345 Avenue of the Americas, 30th Fl.
New York, NY 10105
(212) 843-8000

The Ruder Finn Group
301 East 57th Street
New York, NY 10022
(212) 593-6400

Sandhaus Associates, Inc.
6 East 45th Street, Ste. 1100
New York, NY 10017
(212) 490-4938

Savvy Partners, Inc.
104 West 29th Street, 10th fl.
New York, NY 10001
(212) 244-2660

SCG Promotions Ltd.
124 East 40th Street
New York, NY 10016
(212) 867-2210

Schwartz Public Relations
Associates, Inc.
23 East 22nd Street
New York, NY 10010
(212) 677-8700

Serino Coyne
1515 Broadway, 36th fl.
New York, NY 10036
(212) 626-2700

**Seymour, Nathan & Ozwald
Advertising (SN&O)**
200 West 58th Street, Ste. 2C
New York, NY 10019
(212) 888-1009

Sharpe Partners
134 Fifth Avenue, 3rd fl.
New York, NY 10011
(212) 366-4123

Shepardson Stern & Kaminsky
568 Broadway, 11th fl.
New York, NY 10012
(212) 274-9500

Sherwood Advertising, Inc.
15 West 39th Street
New York, NY 10018
(212) 575-6323

Sound Communications, Inc.
38 East 32nd Street, 6th fl.
New York, NY 10016
(212) 489-1122

Spectrum Marketing, Inc.
127 West 26th Street, 4th fl.
New York, NY 10001
(212) 627-0400

Spier NY
460 Park Avenue South
New York, NY 10016
(212) 679-4441

Spring, O'Brien & Co., Inc.
50 West 23rd Street, 11th fl.
New York, NY 10010
(212) 620-7100

Strategic Domain, Inc.
307 Seventh Avenue, 24th fl.
New York, NY 10001
(212) 812-1900

Stubs Communications Company
226 West 47th Street
New York, NY 10036
(212) 398-8370

**Sudler/Hennessey New York/
Worldwide Headquarters**
230 Park Avenue South, 10th fl.
New York, NY 10003-1566
(212) 614-4100

Team Nash, Inc.
305 Second Avenue
New York, NY 10003
(212) 376-0055

Total Communications Group
122 East 42nd Street
New York, NY 10168
(212) 949-3400

Triton Advertising, Inc.
15 West 44th Street
New York, NY 10036
(212) 840-3040

United Media
200 Madison Avenue, 4th fl.
New York, NY 10016
(212) 293-8500

Uniworld Group, Inc.
100 Avenue of the Americas
New York, NY 10013
(212) 219-1600

Urban Communications
38 West 39th Street, 5th fl.
New York, NY 10018
(212) 997-9699

Vanguard Communications
1120 Avenue of the Americas
New York, NY 10036
(212) 626-6751

Vertical Mix Marketing, Inc.
2 Park Avenue, 14th fl.
New York, NY 10016-9393
(212) 532-6600

Vital Marketing Group
185 Madison Avenue, 11th fl.
New York, NY 10016
(212) 447-5550

Weber Shandwick Worldwide
622 Third Avenue
New York, NY 10017
(646) 658-8000

Don Wise & Co, Inc.
219 East 49th Street
New York, NY 10017
(212) 596-0200

Worldwide Xceed Group, Inc.
233 Broadway
New York, NY 10279
(212) 553-2000

WPI Advertising
121 West 27th Street
New York, NY 10001
(212) 633-2660

Yard Interactive
462 Seventh Avenue, 19th fl.
New York, NY 10018
(212) 244-5540

Young & Rubicam, Inc.
285 Madison Avenue
New York, NY 10017
(212) 210-3000

Ziccardi & Partners, Inc.
1700 Broadway, 35th fl.
New York, NY 10019
(212) 767-1100

LOS ANGELES AGENCIES

Ad Americas
865 South Figueroa, 12th Flr.
Los Angeles, CA 90017
(213) 688-7250

Admarketing, Inc.
1801 Century Park East, Ste. 2000
Los Angeles, CA 90067
(310) 203-8400

Adville/USA
5900 Wilshire Boulevard, Ste. 2400
Los Angeles, CA 90036
(213) 386-8280

Arnold Worldwide
11755 Wilshire Boulevard, Ste. 800
Los Angeles, CA 90025
(310) 960-9099

Bender/Helper Impact, Inc.
11500 Olympic Boulevard, Ste. 655
Los Angeles, CA 90064
(310) 473-4147

Brierly & Partners
5700 Wilshire Boulevard, Ste. 300
Los Angeles, CA 90036
(323) 932-7272

Consolidated Advertising Directors, Inc.
8060 Melrose Avenue
Los Angeles, CA 90046
(323) 653-8060

Creative Domain, Inc.
9000 Sunset Boulevard, 9th Flr.
Los Angeles, CA 90069
(310) 845-8400

DDB Worldwide
11606 Wilshire Boulevard
Los Angeles, CA 90025
(310) 996-5700

Duncan & Associates
11812 San Vincente Boulevard, Ste. 400
Los Angeles, CA 90049
(310) 491-1111

E Squared, Inc.
12301 Wilshire Boulevard, Ste. 305
Los Angeles, CA 90025
(310) 442-3004

Franklyn Agency
1010 Hammond Street, #312
Los Angeles, CA 90069
(323) 272-6080

Frederiksen Group- West Coast, Inc.
10474 Santa Monica Boulevard, Ste. 308
Los Angeles, CA 90025
(310) 662-0220

Gould Advertising, Inc.
2130 Mandeville Canyon Road
Los Angeles, CA 90049-1825
(310) 476-3262

Grey Worldwide
6100 Wilshire Boulevard
Los Angeles, CA 90048
(323) 936-6060

Hamon Associates
6380 Wilshire Boulevard, Ste. 1615
Los Angeles, CA 90048
(323) 653-6073

Horlick Advertising
11300 West Olympic Boulevard, Ste. 700
Los Angeles, CA 90064
(310) 473-6662

Klein Mickaelian Partners
1888 Century Park East, Ste. 1104
Los Angeles, CA 90067-1715
(310) 556-0500

Lee & Associates, Inc.
145 South Fairfax Avenue, Ste. 301
Los Angeles, CA 90036
(323) 938-3300

Marchese Communications Inc.
West Washington Boulevard
Los Angeles, CA 90066
(310) 578-5477

Media Partners Corporation
5670 Wilshire Boulevard, Ste. 1550
Los Angeles, CA 90036
(310) 268-0222

Mendelsohn/Zein Advertising, Inc.
Westwood Gateway
11111 Santa Monica Boulevard, 21st Flr.
Los Angeles, CA 90025-3356
(310) 444-9698

Motivational Incentives
8544 Sunset Boulevard
Los Angeles, CA 90069
(310) 659-3700

Muse Cordero Chen & Partners
6100 Wilshire Boulevard, Ste. 1600
Los Angeles, CA 90048
(323) 954-1655

New-Venture Advertising, Inc.
PO Box 64607
Los Angeles, CA 90064
(818) 906-7878

Park & Foster, Inc.
3596 Beverly Boulevard
Los Angeles, CA 90004
(213) 383-2600

Reckas & Franke Advertising, Inc.
1801 Century Park East, Ste. 1820
Los Angeles, CA 90067
(310) 545-1300

Rogers & Cowan, Inc.
1888 Century Park East, Ste. 500
Los Angeles, CA 90067-1709
(310) 201-8800

Ross Advertising, Inc.
3435 Wilshire Boulevard #2605
Los Angeles, CA 90010
(213) 389-1011

Round2 Communications, LLC
12400 Wilshire Boulevard, Ste. 370
Los Angeles, CA 90025
(310) 571-1823

Russell Gordon Communications
3600 Wilshire Boulevard #428
Los Angeles, CA 90010
(213) 738-5300

Saeshe Advertising
1055 West 7th Street, Ste. 2150
Los Angeles, CA 90017
(213) 683-2100

Sussa Miller
11606 Wilshire Boulevard, 16th Flr.
Los Angeles, CA 90025
(310) 392-9666

Universal Communications, Inc.
11500 Olympic Boulevard, Ste. 400
Los Angeles, CA 90064
(310) 444-3012

Urge Public Relations
6300 Wilshire Boulevard, Ste. 1750
Los Angeles, CA 90048
(323) 762-1600

WPA Communications, Inc.
2021 Pontius Avenue
Los Angeles, CA 90025
(310) 473-6033

XCEED, Inc.
11755 Wilshire Boulevard, 19th Flr.
Los Angeles, CA 90025
(310) 473-3000

Zenith Media Services, Inc.
6300 Wilshire Boulevard, Ste. 1410
Los Angeles, CA 90048
(323) 782-5100

CHICAGO AGENCIES

BBDO Chicago
410 North Michigan Avenue
Chicago, IL 60611
(312) 337-7860

Becker & Company
1333 North Kingsbury Avenue
Chicago, IL 60622
(312) 587-7799

Bender, Browning, Dolby
& Sanderson Advertising
444 North Michigan Avenue,
Ste. 1400
Chicago, IL 60611
(312) 644-9600

Lou Beres
& Associates, Inc.
410 North Michigan Avenue
Chicago, IL 60611
(312) 670-0470

Campbell Mithun-Chicago
676 North Saint Clair
Chicago, IL 60611
(312)988-2000

Carat (Chicago)
401 North Michigan Avenue 14th fl.
Chicago, IL 60611
(312) 384-4500

Chase Ehrenberg & Rosene, Inc.
230 East Ohio Street, Ste. 306
Chicago, IL 60611
(312) 943-3737

Chicago Creative Partnership
314 West Superior Street
Chicago, IL 60610
(312) 335-4330

CMYK & Beyond LLC
10 East Ontario Street, #1705
Chicago, IL 60611
(312) 943-9232

Coil Counts Ford & Cheney, Inc.
150 East Huron Street, Ste. 1250
Chicago, IL 60611
(312) 649-6300

The Corbett Healthcare Group
211 East Chicago Avenue
Chicago, IL 60611
(312) 664-5310

Cramer-Krasselt
225 North Michigan Avenue
Chicago, IL 60601
(312) 616-9600

Creative Marketing Resource, Inc.
919 North Michigan Avenue Ste. 600
Chicago, IL 60611
(312) 943-6266

Davis Harrison Dion
333 North Michigan Avenue Ste. 2300
Chicago, IL 60601
(312) 332-0808

Dawson Hackley Advertising
1000 West Diversey Pkwy.
Ste. 234
Chicago, IL 60614
(773) 871-2930

Donahoe Purohit Miller, Inc.
311 South Wacker Dr.,
Ste. 2350
Chicago, IL 60606
(312) 341-8100

Duncan & Associates Chicago
225 West Ohio Street, #280
Chicago, IL 60610
(312) 670-3123

Ebel Dunnell Merrick
318 West Adams
Chicago, IL 60606
(312) 364-4900

Esdale Associates, Inc.
434 West Armitage Avenue, Unit C
Chicago, IL 60614
(773) 755-7610

Euro RSCG McCounnaghy Tatham
36 East Grand Avenue
Chicago, IL 60611-3506
(312) 337-5930

Euro RSCG Tatham Interaction
36 East Grand Avenue
Chicago, IL 60611-3506
(312) 337-4400

Eyehand Interactive, Inc.
213 West Institute Place, Ste. 712
Chicago, IL 60610
(312) 787-7773

Fairman, Schmidt & Hurley, Inc.
500 North Michigan Avenue Ste. 400
Chicago, IL 60611
(312) 464-9797

GCI Dragonette
205 West Wacker Drive, Ste. 2200
Chicago, IL 60606
(312) 424-5300

GDM
350 West Hubbard Street
Chicago, IL 60610
(312) 222-0025

Gelia Chicago
8501 West Higgins Road, Ste. 430
Chicago, IL 60631
(773) 714-1240

Goble & Associates
800 South Wells Street, Ste. 200
Chicago, IL 60607
(312) 803-1900

GRP Media, Inc.
One East Wacker Drive, Ste. 2510
Chicago, IL 60601
(312) 836-0995

Hamilton Communications Group, Inc.
401 East Illinois Street, Ste. 500
Chicago, IL 60611
(312) 321-5000

Hear Spot Run Marketing
311 West Superior Street
Ste. 509
Chicago, IL 60602
(312) 944-7833

Huwen & Davies, Inc.
430 West Erie Street
Chicago, IL 60610
(312) 440-9500

Jacobs & Clevenger, Inc.
401 North Wabash Avenue,
Ste. 620
Chicago, IL 60611-5647
(312) 894-3000

Jerry & Joan Creative
233 East Wacker Drive,
Ste. 4011
Chicago, IL 60601
(312) 938-1013

Jordan Tamarz Caruso Advertising, Inc.
JTC Bldg.
1419 North Wells Street
Chicago, IL 60610-1395
(312) 951-2000

Kelly, Scott and Madison
35 East Wacker Drive,
Chicago, IL 60601
(312) 977-0772

Killian & Company Advertising
North Pier
455 East Illinois Street, Ste. 475
Chicago, IL 60611-5309
(312) 936-0050

Kimmel & Co.
401 North Racine Avenue
Chicago, IL 60622
(312) 666-1123

LCI Chicago
515 North State Street
Chicago, IL 60610
(312) 836-9886

Lubow Advertising, Inc.
226 East Ontario Street,
Chicago, IL 60611
(312) 280-0127

MacDonald Media/Chicago
401 North Michigan, 12th Fl.
Chicago, IL 60611
(312) 840-8252

Magnani Continuum Marketing
200 South Michigan Avenue,
Ste. 1616
Chicago, IL 60604
(312) 957-0770

Matrix Partners, Ltd.
566 West Adams, Ste. 720
Chicago, IL 60661
(312) 648-9972

Michael Meyers & Associates, Inc.
500 North Michigan Avenue,
Ste. 1600
Chicago, IL 60611
(312) 661-0055

MGS Consulting, Inc.
3639 North Harding Avenue
Chicago, IL 60618
(773)583-2600

Mobium Creative Group
The Merchandise Mart,
Ste. 2000
Chicago, IL 60654
(312) 527-0500

Ogilvy & Mather
111 East Wacker Drive,
Chicago, IL 60601-4208
(312) 856-8200

Pragmaton
211 East Chicago Avenue
Chicago, IL 60611
(312) 664-5310

Publicis & Hal Riney Chicago
224 South Michigan Avenue
Chicago, IL 60604
(312) 697-5700

Tom Reilly Advertising, Inc.
142 East Ontario Street, 13th Fl.
Chicago, IL 60611
(312) 787-2330

The Rosen Group
640 North LaSalle Street, Ste. 555
Chicago, IL 60610
(312) 951-1900
401 North Wabash Street, Ste. 600
Chicago, IL 60611
(312) 464-1666

Slack Barshinger & Partners, Inc.
444 North Michigan Avenue, 9th Fl.
Chicago, IL 60611
(312) 527-0777

Upshot
303 East Wacker Drive, Ste. 2300
Chicago, IL 60601
(312) 943-0900

**Washington Daniel
Advertising, Inc.**
980 North Michigan Avenue, Ste.
1180
Chicago, IL 60611
(312) 951-5366

Zenith Media Services
875 North Michigan Avenue,
Ste. 2130
Chicago, IL 60611
(312) 278-8800

Pamela Lewis has talked for just about every kind of creature in commercial/character/ cartoon voice-overs, from a chocolate-deprived wimp for Hershey's, to the Evil Sorceress for Nintendo video games, to some very animated Ritz Bits crackers. As one of New York's busiest "dialogue replacement" specialists, she's put hysteria, conversation and special effects into the mouths of hundreds of screen actors, and has been the "baby voice" in many national commercials. Pamela has long been established as one of the voice-over industry's most respected cartoon/character/looping coaches, and travels nationwide giving her very popular *Talking Funny for Money* workshops.